Welcome

30-MINUTE DIABETIC COOKBOOK

Welcome Home
30-MINUTE DIABETIC COOKBOOK

QUICK & EASY HEALTHY RECIPES

Hope Comerford

Photos by Bonnie Matthews

Good Books

New York, New York

Good Books books may be purchased in bulk at special discounts for sales promotion, corporate gifts, fund-raising, or educational purposes. Special editions can also be created to specifications. For details, contact the Special Sales Department, Good Books, 307 West 36th Street, 11th Floor, New York, NY 10018 or info@skyhorsepublishing.com.

Good Books is an imprint of Skyhorse Publishing, Inc.®, a Delaware corporation.

Visit our website at www.goodbooks.com.

10 9 8 7 6 5 4 3 2 1

Library of Congress Cataloging-in-Publication Data is available on file.

Cover design by Kai Texel
Cover photo by Bonnie Matthews

Print ISBN: 978-1-68099-953-2
Ebook ISBN: 978-1-68099-958-7

Printed in China

The information provided in this book is designed to provide accurate and authoritative information with respect to the subject matter covered. This book is not meant to be used, nor should it be used, to diagnose or treat any medical condition. For diagnosis or treatment of any medical problem, consult your own physician. While every attempt is made to provide accurate information, the authors or publisher cannot be held accountable for any errors, omissions, or material which is no longer up to date.

Table of Contents

My Brother's Black Bean Salad, page 160

About Welcome Home 30-Minute Diabetic Cookbook!

Even those with special dietary needs deserve to have an easy, homemade meal, ready to go quickly, and without much thought. When you're diabetic, it is important to manage your calorie, carb, fat, and sodium counts. Taking that into account, following every recipe in this book, you will find its Exchange List Values, which list carbs, fats, starches, etc. and the Basic Nutritional Values as well. Our hope is that providing this information for all 127 recipes in this book, it will help ease some of the stress you might feel daily when trying to find recipes that will work for you.

In this cookbook, you will find recipes for main courses and sides like Lemony Quinoa and Chickpea Bowls, Shrimp Stir-Fry, Quesadilla Casserole, BLT Salad, Sweet Potato Puree, and Apple Coleslaw. There are also a variety of breakfast, appetizer, and snack options like Greek Eggs, Tofu Lettuce Wraps, and Pineapple Cheese Dip. You'll even find delicious desserts to safely enjoy like Apple-Walnut Cookies and Chocolate Peanut Butter Fudge.

As you begin journeying through this book, I always suggest reading it from cover to cover. I can't tell you the good recipes I've passed on in the past by not following this advice. Don't become overwhelmed. Bookmark, or dog-ear the pages of the recipes that you think your family would enjoy the most, can be made with ingredients you have around the house, or fit with their dietary needs. Then, when you've looked at everything, go back to those marked pages and narrow it down. Make yourself a grocery list and grab what you don't already have. Voilà! You're ready to get cooking!

Calculating the Nutritional Analyses

If the number of servings is given as a range, we used the higher number to do the nutritional analyses calculations.

The nutritional analysis for each recipe includes all ingredients except those labeled "optional," those listed as "to taste," or those calling for a "dash." If an ingredient is listed with a second choice, the first choice was used in the analysis. If a range is given for the amount of an ingredient, the first number was used. Foods listed as "serve with" at the end of a recipe, or accompanying foods listed without an amount, were not included in the recipe's analysis. In recipes calling for cooked rice, pasta, or other grains, the analysis is based on the starch being prepared without added salt or fat, unless indicated otherwise in the recipe. Please note, too, that the nutritional analyses do not cover the ingredients included in the Tips, Variations, and Serving Suggestions that follow some of the recipes.

The analyses were done assuming that meats were trimmed of all visible fat, and that skin was removed from poultry, before being cooked.

Tips for Healthier, Happier Eating

How to Plan Healthy Meals

Healthy meal planning is an important part of diabetes care. If you have diabetes, you should have a meal plan specifying what, when, and how much you should eat. Work with a registered dietitian to create a meal plan that is right for you. A typical meal plan covers your meals and snacks and includes a variety of foods. Here are some popular meal-planning tools:

1. **An exchange list** is a list of foods that are grouped together because they share similar carbohydrate, protein, and fat content. Any food on an exchange list may be substituted for any other food on the same list. A meal plan that uses exchange lists will tell you the number of exchanges (or food choices) you can eat at each meal or snack. You then choose the foods that add up to those exchanges.

2. **Carbohydrate counting** is useful because carbohydrates are the main nutrient in food that affects blood glucose. When you count carbohydrates, you simply count up the carbohydrates in the foods you eat, which helps you manage your blood glucose levels. To find the carbohydrate content of a food, check the Nutrition Facts label on foods or ask your dietitian for help. Carbohydrate counting is especially helpful for people with diabetes who take insulin to help manage their blood glucose.

3. **The "Create Your Plate" method** helps people with diabetes put together meals with evenly distributed carbohydrate content and correct portion sizes. This is one of the easiest meal-planning options because it does not require any special tools—all you need is a plate. Fill half of your plate with non-starchy vegetables, such as spinach, carrots, cabbage, green beans, or broccoli. Fill one-quarter of the plate with starchy foods, such as rice, pasta, beans, or peas. Fill the final quarter of your plate with meat or a meat substitute, such as cheese with less than 3 grams of fat per ounce, cottage cheese, or egg substitute. For a balanced meal, add a serving of low-fat or nonfat milk and a serving of fruit.

No matter which tool you use to plan your meals, having a meal plan in place can help you manage your blood glucose levels, improve your cholesterol levels, and maintain a healthy

Flounder Zucchini Bundles, page 126

blood pressure and a healthy weight. When you're able to do that, you're helping to control—or avoid—diabetes.

Learning Portion Control

Portion control is an important part of healthier eating. Weighing and measuring your foods helps you become familiar with reasonable portions and can make a difference of several hundred calories each day. You want to weigh and measure your foods frequently when you begin following a healthy eating plan. The more you practice weighing and measuring, the easier it will become to estimate portion sizes accurately.

You'll want to have certain portion-control tools on hand when you're weighing and measuring your foods. Remember, the teaspoons and tablespoons in your silverware set won't give you exact measurements. Here's what goes into your portion-control toolbox:

- Measuring spoons for ½ teaspoon, 1 teaspoon, ½ tablespoon, and 1 tablespoon
- A see-through 1-cup measuring cup with markings at ¼, ⅓, ½, ⅔, and ¾ cup
- Measuring cups for dry ingredients, including ¼, ⅓, ½, and 1 cup.

You may already have most of these in your kitchen. Keep them on your counter—you are more likely to use these tools if you can see them. Get an inexpensive food scale for foods that are measured in ounces, such as fresh produce, baked goods, meats, and cheese. When you're weighing meat, poultry, and seafood, keep in mind that you will need more than 3 ounces of raw meat to produce a 3-ounce portion of cooked meat. For example, it takes 4 ounces of raw, boneless meat—or 5 ounces of raw meat with the bone—to produce 3 cooked ounces. About 4½ ounces of raw chicken (with the bone and skin) yields 3 ounces cooked. Remember to remove the skin from the chicken before eating it.

There are other easy ways to control your portions at home in addition to weighing and measuring:

- Eat on smaller plates and bowls so that small portions look normal, not skimpy.
- Use a measuring cup to serve food to easily determine how much you're serving and eating.
- Measure your drinking glasses and bowls, so you know how much you're drinking or eating when you fill them.
- Avoid serving your meals family-style because leaving large serving dishes on the table can lead to second helpings and overeating.
- Keep portion sizes in mind while shopping. When you buy meat, fish, or poultry, purchase only what you need for your meal.

When you're away from home, your eyes and hands become your portion-control tools. You can use your hand to estimate teaspoons, tablespoons, ounces, and cups. The tip of your thumb is about 1 teaspoon; your whole thumb equals roughly 1 tablespoon. Two fingers lengthwise are about an ounce, and 3 ounces is about the size of a palm. You can use your fist to measure in cups. A tight fist is about half a cup, whereas a loose fist or cupped hand is closer to a cup. These guidelines are true for most women's hands, but some men's hands are much larger. The palm of a man's hand is often the equivalent of about 5 ounces. Check the size of your hand in relation to various portions.

Remember that the more you weigh and measure your foods at home, the easier it will be to estimate portions on the road.

Controlling your portions when you eat at a restaurant can be difficult. Try to stay away from menu items with portion descriptors that are large, such as "giant," "supreme," "extra-large," "double," "triple," "king-size," and "super." Don't fall for deals in which the "value" is to serve you more food so that you can save money. Avoid all-you-can-eat restaurants and buffets.

You can split, share, or mix-and-match menu items to get what you want to eat in the correct portions. If you know that the portions you'll be served will be too large, ask for a take-home container when you place your order and put half of your food away before you start eating.

Gradually, as you become better at portion control, you can weigh and measure your foods less frequently. If you feel like you are correctly estimating your portions, just weigh and measure once a week, or even once a month, to check that your portions are still accurate. A good habit to get into is to "calibrate" your portion-control memory at least once a month, so you don't start overestimating your portion sizes. Always weigh and measure new foods and foods that you tend to overestimate.

Frequently Asked Questions about Diabetes and Food

1. Do people with diabetes have to eat a special diet?

No, they should eat the same foods that are healthy for everyone—whole grains, vegetables, fruit, and small portions of lean meat. Like everyone else, people with diabetes should eat breakfast, lunch, and dinner and not put off eating until dinnertime. By then, you are ravenous and will eat too much. This sends blood sugar levels soaring in people with diabetes, and doesn't allow them to feel hungry for breakfast the next morning.

Shrimp & Zucchini Sauté, page 134

2. Can people with diabetes eat sugar?

Yes, they can. Sugar is just another carbohydrate to the body. All carbohydrates, whether they come from dessert, breads, or carrots, raise blood sugar. An equal serving of brownie and of baked potato raise your blood sugar the same amount. If you know that a rise in blood sugar is coming, it is wise to focus on the size of the serving. The question of "how much sugar is too much?" has to be answered by each one of us. No one who wants to be healthy eats a lot of sugar.

3. What natural substances are good sugar substitutes? Are artificial sweeteners safe for people with diabetes?

Honey, agave nectar, maple syrup, brown sugar, and white sugar all contain about the same amount of calories and have a similar effect on your blood glucose levels. All of these sweeteners are a source of carbohydrates and will raise blood glucose quickly.

If you have diabetes, you can use these sweeteners sparingly if you work them into your meal plan. Be aware of portion sizes and the carbohydrate content of each sweetener:

- 1 tablespoon honey = about 64 calories, 17 grams of carbohydrate
- 1 tablespoon brown sugar = about 52 calories, 13 grams of carbohydrate
- 1 tablespoon white sugar = about 48 calories, 13 grams of carbohydrate
- 1 tablespoon agave nectar = about 45 calories, 12 grams of carbohydrate
- 1 tablespoon maple syrup = about 52 calories, 13 grams of carbohydrate
- 1 packet of artificial sweetener = about 4 calories, <1 gram of carbohydrate

Artificial sweeteners are a low-calorie, low-carb option. Because they are chemically modified to be sweeter than regular sugar, only a small amount is needed to sweeten foods and drinks. There are several different artificial sweeteners available under various brand names: stevia, aspartame, acesulfame-K, saccharin, or sucralose. With the direction of your health care provider, these may be safe options for people with diabetes when used in moderate amounts.

4. How many grams of carbohydrates should someone with diabetes eat per day? How many at each meal?

This is a very common question. About 45–60 grams of carbohydrates per meal is a good starting point when you are carb-counting. If you follow that recommendation, you will be eating a total of 135–180 grams of carbohydrates per day. However, some people may need more, and some may need less. Talk with your health care team to create an individualized meal plan to help you meet your health goals.

5. What types of fruit can I eat? Is canned or fresh fruit better for people with diabetes?

You can eat any type of fruit if you work it into your meal plan. Fruits are loaded with vitamins, minerals, and fiber. Fresh, canned, or frozen fruit without added sugars are all good options. You get a similar amount of nutrients from each. When you buy canned fruit, be sure the fruit has been canned in water or juice—not in syrup.

Fruit is nutritious, but it is not a "free food." The following portions have about 15 grams of carbohydrates:

- 1 small piece of whole fruit such as a small apple, small orange, or kiwifruit
- ½ cup of frozen or canned fruit
- ¾–1 cup of fresh berries or melon
- ⅓–½ cup 100% no-sugar-added fruit juice
- 2 tablespoons of dried fruit

6. Besides meat, what can I eat to make sure I get enough protein?

There are many protein sources. Proteins that are low in saturated and trans fats are the best options. Choose lean sources of protein like these:

- Eggs, egg whites, and egg substitutes
- Vegetarian proteins: beans, soy products, veggie burgers, nuts, and seeds
- Low-fat or nonfat dairy products
- Fish and shellfish
- Poultry without the skin
- Cheeses with 3 grams of fat or less per ounce
- When you do eat meat, choose lean cuts

People with diabetes can follow a vegetarian or vegan diet. Plant-based diets that include some animal products like eggs and milk can be a healthy option. However, animal products are not necessary. A mix of soy products, vegetables, fruits, beans, and whole grains provides plenty of protein and nutrients.

7. Why should I eat whole grains instead of refined grains?

Even a food made with 100% whole wheat flour will raise your blood glucose levels. All grains—whole or not—affect blood glucose because they contain carbohydrates. However, you shouldn't completely avoid starchy foods. People with diabetes need some carbohydrates in their diet.

Whole grains are a healthy starch option because they contain fiber, vitamins, and minerals. Choose whole wheat or whole-grain foods over those made with refined grains, but watch your portion sizes.

8. Can people with diabetes eat potatoes and sweet potatoes?

Yes! Starchy vegetables are healthy sources of carbohydrates. They also provide you with important nutrients like potassium, fiber, and vitamin C. You can include them in your meal plan as part of a balanced meal. Just pay attention to portion sizes and avoid unhealthy toppings. If you are carb-counting, remember that there are about 15 grams of carbohydrates in:

- ½ cup of mashed potatoes
- ½ cup of boiled potatoes
- ¼ of a large baked potato with the skin

9. Without salt and fat, food tastes bland. What can I do?

When you are preparing healthy foods, try to limit added fats and extra salt. Look for recipes that use herbs (fresh or dried) and spices for flavor instead. There are many spice blends available in the baking aisle at the grocery store—choose salt-free blends. Other healthy ways to flavor your foods include:

- Squeezing lemon or lime juice on vegetables, fish, rice, or pasta
- Using onion and garlic to flavor dishes
- Baking meats with sugar-free barbecue sauce or any low-fat marinade
- Adding low-fat, low-calorie condiments, such as mustard, salsa, balsamic vinegar, or hot sauce

10. Are gluten-free products okay for people with diabetes to eat?

About 1 percent of the total population has celiac disease, which is an allergy to gluten—a protein found in wheat, rye, and barley. About 10 percent of people with type 1 diabetes also have celiac disease. People with celiac disease or gluten intolerance should follow a gluten-free diet. However, unless you have one of these conditions, following a gluten-free diet is unnecessary and can make meal planning more difficult. Gluten-free products may contain more grams of carbohydrates per serving than regular products. For example, gluten-free bread can have twice as many grams of carbohydrates as whole wheat bread. You can use gluten-free products and recipes, but just be sure to check the carbohydrate content and calories.

Appetizers & Snacks

Easy Turkey Roll-Ups

Rhoda Atzeff, Lancaster, PA

Makes 6 servings, 2 roll-ups per serving

Prep. Time: 10 minutes

3 (6-inch) whole wheat tortillas

3 Tbsp. reduced-fat chive and onion cream cheese

12 slices deli shaved 97%-fat-free turkey breast, 6 oz. total

¾ cup shredded lettuce

1. Spread tortillas with cream cheese. Top with turkey. Place lettuce on bottom halves of tortillas; roll up.

2. Cut each into 4 pieces and lay flat to serve.

Calories: 177
Fat: 6 g
Saturated Fat: 3 g
Carbohydrates: 21 g
Fiber: 4 g
Sodium: 536 mg
Protein: 9 g
Cholesterol: 17 mg

STOVETOP

Tofu Lettuce Wraps

Hope Comerford, Clinton Township, MI

Makes about 12 wraps

Prep. Time: 10 minutes   Cooking Time: 15–20 minutes

32 oz. meatless crumbles

4 cloves garlic, minced

½ cup minced sweet yellow onion

8-oz. can sliced water chestnuts, drained, rinsed, chopped

3 green onions, sliced

4 Tbsp. low-sodium soy sauce

1 Tbsp. no-sugar-added crunchy peanut butter

1 tsp. rice wine vinegar

1 tsp. sesame oil

¼ tsp. kosher salt

¼ tsp. red pepper flakes

¼ tsp. black pepper

12 good-sized pieces of iceberg lettuce, rinsed and patted dry

1. In a nonstick skillet, combine the meatless crumbles, garlic, and yellow onion. Sauté until onion is slightly translucent.

2. Add in the water chestnuts and green onions and continue to sauté.

3. Combine soy sauce, peanut butter, vinegar, sesame oil, salt, red pepper flakes, and black pepper in small bowl, then pour over contents of nonstick pan. Let simmer for about 5 minutes.

4. Serve a good spoonful on each piece of iceberg lettuce.

Serving suggestion:
Garnish with diced red bell pepper and diced green onion.

Calories: 98

Fat: 5 g

Saturated Fat: 1 g

Carbohydrates: 8 g

Fiber: 2 g

Sodium: 276 mg

Protein: 8 g

Cholesterol: 0 mg

Shrimp Appetizer Platter

Tammy Smith, Dorchester, WI

Makes 5 cups, 20 servings, ¼ cup per serving

Prep. Time: 15 minutes

8 oz. fat-free cream cheese, softened

½ cup fat-free sour cream

¼ cup reduced-fat mayonnaise

4-oz. can broken shrimp, rinsed and drained

1 cup cocktail sauce

2 cups reduced-fat shredded cheddar cheese

1 bell pepper, chopped

1 tomato, chopped

3 green onions, chopped

1. Beat together cream cheese, sour cream and mayonnaise. Spread on bottom of a 12-inch platter.

2. Layer rest of ingredients in order given.

3. Cover and chill. Serve with crackers.

Calories: 90

Fat: 1 g

Saturated Fat: 0 g

Carbohydrates: 8 g

Fiber: 0 g

Sodium: 522 mg

Protein: 11 g

Cholesterol: 19 mg

NO-COOK

Easy Layered Taco Dip

Lindsey Spencer, Morrow, OH
Jenny R. Unternahrer, Wayland, IA

Makes 10 servings

Prep. Time: 15 minutes

8 oz. fat-free cream cheese, softened

8 oz. fat-free sour cream

8 oz. taco sauce or salsa

4 cups shredded lettuce

I cup chopped tomato

Chopped green pepper, *optional*

I cup reduced-fat shredded
Mexi-blend cheese

Whole-grain tortilla chips

1. Blend cream cheese and sour cream until smooth. Spread in bottom of a 9 × 13-inch dish.

2. Layer taco sauce over sour cream mixture, then lettuce, tomato, and cheese.

3. Serve with whole-grain tortilla chips.

Tip:
If you can, add the lettuce, tomato, and cheese at the last minute so the lettuce doesn't get soggy.
—Jenny R. Unternahrer, Wayland, IA

Calories: 234
Fat: I I g
Saturated Fat: 3 g
Carbohydrates: 28 g
Fiber: 3 g
Sodium: 536 mg
Protein: I3 g
Cholesterol: I9 mg

Mexican Corn Dip

Janie Steele, Moore, OK

Makes 28 servings, about ¼ cup per serving

Prep. Time: 10 minutes

8 oz. fat-free sour cream

1 cup light mayonnaise

2 (11-oz.) cans Mexican-style corn

4 green onions, chopped

4½-oz. can chopped green chilies

1¼ cups reduced-fat shredded cheddar cheese

1–3 jalapeño peppers, seeds removed, chopped

1. Mix ingredients together.

2. Serve with dippers of your choice.

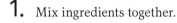

Calories: 64

Fat: 3 g

Saturated Fat: 0.5 g

Carbohydrates: 6 g

Fiber: 0.5 g

Sodium: 173 mg

Protein: 4 g

Cholesterol: 6 mg

Pineapple Salsa

NO-COOK

Lorraine Stutzman Amstutz, Akron, PA

Makes 2½ cups, 10 servings, ¼ cup per serving

Prep. Time: 30 minutes

1½ cups fresh pineapple
1 cup cucumber
¼ cup red onion
2–4 tsp. minced jalapeño
1 tsp. garlic
2 Tbsp. fresh cilantro
¼ cup lime juice
1 tsp. grated lime peel
1 tsp. sugar
¼ tsp. salt

1. Pulse ingredients together in food processor until just chopped.

Tip:
If you don't have a food processor, simply chop the pineapple, cucumber, onion, jalapeño, garlic, and cilantro. Combine with lime, grated lime peel, sugar, and salt.

Calories: 20
Fat: 0 g
Saturated Fat: 0.0 g
Carbohydrates: 5 g
Fiber: 1 g
Sodium: 49 mg
Protein: 0 g
Cholesterol: 0 mg

Pineapple Cheese Dip

Mamie Christopherson, Rio Rancho, NM

Makes 36 servings, scant 2 Tbsp. per serving

Prep. Time: 10 minutes

2 (8-oz.) pkg. fat-free cream cheese, softened

8-oz. can no-sugar-added crushed pineapple, drained

2 cups chopped pecans

2 Tbsp. finely chopped onion

1 Tbsp. seasoned salt

1. Soften cream cheese at room temperature. Beat with mixer until fluffy.

2. Add pineapple, pecans, onion, and salt.

Serving suggestion:

Serve with whole-grain crackers.

Variation:

Leave out 1 cup of the pecans. Chill mixture for several hours. Shape into a ball and roll in the reserved pecans.

—Joyce Shackelford, Green Bay, WI

Calories: 55
Fat: 4 g
Saturated Fat: 0.4 g
Carbohydrates: 3 g
Fiber: 1 g
Sodium: 215 mg
Protein: 3 g
Cholesterol: 20 mg

Apple Dippers

Christine Lucke, Aumsville, OR

Makes 8 servings, 2 Tbsp. per serving

Prep. Time: 15 minutes

8 oz. fat-free cream cheese

2 tsp. fat-free milk

⅓ cup brown sugar

Apples for dipping

1. Whip cream cheese, milk, and brown sugar to a smooth, fluffy consistency.

2. Serve with sliced apples for dipping.

Tips:

1. I like Braeburn or Cameo apples.
2. You can use some lemon juice and water to keep the apples from browning, but I just slice right before serving and the Braeburns don't turn brown before they are eaten.

Calories: 101

Fat: 0.5 g

Saturated Fat: 0 g

Carbohydrates: 21 g

Fiber: 2 g

Sodium: 203 mg

Protein: 5 g

Cholesterol: 3 mg

Pretty Fruit Kabobs with Dip

Anya Kauffman, Sheldon, WI

Makes 40 servings, 1 kabob and 2 Tbsp. dip per serving

Prep. Time: 30 minutes

8 oz. Neufchâtel (⅓-less-fat) cream cheese, softened

8-oz. fat-free frozen whipped topping, thawed

6 oz. Walden Farms Marshmallow Dessert Dip

1 tsp. vanilla extract

¼ cup fat-free milk

1 lb. green grapes

1 pineapple, cut in 80 pieces

1 lb. red grapes

1 honeydew, cut in 80 pieces

2 lb. strawberries, cut in 40 pieces

40 (8-inch) skewers

1. Beat cream cheese until fluffy.

2. Fold in whipped topping and marshmallow dessert dip. Add vanilla and milk.

3. Refrigerate until ready to serve.

4. For kabobs, thread green grape, pineapple, red grape, honeydew, strawberry, honeydew, red grape, pineapple, green grape on skewers. Serve.

Calories: 55

Fat: 0 g

Saturated Fat: 0 g

Carbohydrates: 13 g

Fiber: 1 g

Sodium: 49 mg

Protein: 1 g

Cholesterol: 1 mg

INSTANT POT

Insta Popcorn

Hope Comerford, Clinton Township, MI

Makes 5–6 servings

Prep. Time: 1 minute   ♨   Cooking Time: about 5 minutes

2 Tbsp. coconut oil

½ cup popcorn kernels

¼ cup margarine spread, melted, *optional*

Sea salt to taste

1. Set the Instant Pot to Sauté.

2. Melt the coconut oil in the inner pot, then add the popcorn kernels and stir.

3. Press Adjust to bring the temperature up to high.

4. When the corn starts popping, secure the lid on the Instant Pot.

5. When you no longer hear popping, turn off the Instant Pot, remove the lid, and pour the popcorn into a bowl.

6. Top with the optional melted margarine and season the popcorn with sea salt to your liking.

Calories: 161

Fat: 13 g

Saturated Fat: 5 g

Carbohydrates: 13 g

Fiber: 3 g

Sodium: 88 mg

Protein: 2 g

Cholesterol: 0 mg

Breakfasts

Greek Eggs

Rosanne Hankins, Stevensville, MD

Makes 4 servings

Prep. Time: 5 minutes   *Cooking Time: 12–15 minutes*

2 cloves garlic, sliced
¼ cup sliced white onion
1 Tbsp. olive oil
1 lb. fresh chopped spinach
8 eggs, beaten
1 Tbsp. fresh chopped oregano
4 oz. reduced-fat feta cheese

1. In large skillet, sauté garlic and onion in oil for 3–4 minutes.

2. Stir in spinach and let wilt.

3. Pour eggs and oregano into hot skillet.

4. Cook, turning 2–3 times, until eggs are lightly cooked, about 5 minutes.

5. Turn off heat; crumble cheese over top of spinach-egg mixture. Cover and let set for 2 minutes, or until cheese melts into eggs.

Variations:

1. For added color and flavor, stir half a sweet red bell pepper, chopped, into Step 1.
2. For additional flavor, add 1/4 tsp. black or white pepper and 1/8 tsp. salt in Step 3.

Calories: 275
Fat: 19 g
Saturated Fat: 7 g
Carbohydrates: 7 g
Fiber: 3 g
Sodium: 529 mg
Protein: 20 g
Cholesterol: 392 mg

STOVETOP

Eggs à la Shrimp

Willard E. Roth, Elkhart, IN

Makes 6 servings

Prep. Time: 15 minutes ⚜ *Cooking Time: 15 minutes*

1 Tbsp. olive oil

3 green onions with tops, sliced,
or 1 small onion, chopped fine

¼ cup finely chopped celery
with leaves

4 oz. shrimp, frozen or canned

3 Tbsp. + ¼ cup white wine, *divided*

4 large eggs

1 cup egg substitute

4 oz. frozen or fresh peas

¼ tsp. salt

¼ tsp. pepper

Fresh parsley

1. Preheat cast-iron skillet to medium high.

2. Heat oil in skillet. Sauté onions until limp.

3. Add celery and sauté until softened.

4. Add shrimp and 3 Tbsp. white wine. Cover and steam over low heat for 3 minutes.

5. In a medium-sized mixing bowl, toss eggs and egg substitute with ¼ cup white wine. Pour into skillet.

6. Stir in peas and seasonings.

7. Turn heat down or medium low. Stir gently as mixture cooks. Cook just until mixture sets according to your liking.

8. Serve on warm platter surrounded with fresh parsley.

Serving suggestion:
Serve with fresh fruit in season.

Calories: 127

Fat: 6 g

Saturated Fat: 1 g

Carbohydrates: 4 g

Fiber: 1 g

Sodium: 397 mg

Protein: 13 g

Cholesterol: 164 mg

Poached Eggs

Hope Comerford, Clinton Township, MI

Makes 2–4 servings

Prep. Time: 5 minutes   Cooking Time: 2–5 minutes

1 cup water

4 large eggs

1. Place the trivet in the bottom of the inner pot of the Instant Pot and pour in the water.

2. You will need small silicone egg poacher cups that will fit in your Instant Pot to hold the eggs. Spray each silicone cup with nonstick cooking spray.

3. Crack each egg and pour it into the prepared cup.

4. Very carefully place the silicone cups into the Inner Pot so they do not spill.

5. Secure the lid by locking it into place and turn the vent to the sealing position.

6. Push the Steam button and adjust the time—2 minutes for a very runny egg all the way to 5 minutes for a slightly runny egg.

7. When the timer beeps, release the pressure manually and remove the lid, being very careful not to let the condensation in the lid drip into your eggs.

8. Very carefully remove the silicone cups from the inner pot.

9. Carefully remove the poached eggs from each silicone cup and serve immediately.

Calories: 72

Fat: 5 g

Saturated Fat: 1.6 g

Carbohydrates: 0.4 g

Fiber: 0 g

Sodium: 71 mg

Protein: 6 g

Cholesterol: 186 mg

Spinach & Mushroom Frittata

J. B. Miller, Indianapolis, IN

Makes 4 servings

Prep. Time: 5 minutes ⚬ *Cooking Time: 10 minutes*

6 eggs
½ tsp. salt
¼ tsp. black pepper
1 Tbsp. minced fresh basil
3 cloves garlic, minced
1 small shallot, minced
½ lb. sliced baby bella mushrooms
10-oz. bag fresh spinach
¼ cup reduced-fat shredded Gruyère cheese
1 cup water

1. In a bowl, beat the eggs, salt, and pepper.

2. Gently fold in the basil, garlic, shallot, mushrooms, spinach, and cheese.

3. Spray a 7-inch round pan with nonstick cooking spray, then pour in the egg/vegetable/cheese mixture.

4. Pour the water into the bottom of the inner pot of the Instant Pot.

5. Place the 7-inch round pan on top of the trivet and slowly lower it into the Instant Pot using the handles.

6. Secure the lid and set the valve to sealing.

7. Set the Instant Pot to Manual and set the cooking time to 10 minutes.

8. When the cooking time is over, let the pressure release naturally, then remove the lid and remove the trivet and pan carefully with oven mitts.

9. Cut into 4 slices and serve warm.

Calories: 173
Fat: 10 g
Saturated Fat: 4 g
Carbohydrates: 6 g
Fiber: 2 g
Sodium: 422 mg
Protein: 15 g
Cholesterol: 288 mg

Oatmeal Morning

Barbara Forrester Landis, Lititz, PA

Makes 6 servings

Prep. Time: 5 minutes   Cooking Time: 4 minutes

2 cups water, divided

2 cups uncooked steel-cut oats

1 cup dried cranberries

1 cup walnuts

½ tsp. salt

1 Tbsp. cinnamon

2 cups fat-free milk

1. Place the steaming rack into the inner pot of the Instant Pot and pour in the 1 cup of water.

2. In an approximately 7-cup heat-safe baking dish, add all ingredients and stir.

3. Place the dish on top of the steaming rack; close the lid and secure it to a locking position.

4. Be sure the vent is set to sealing, then set the Instant Pot for 4 minutes on Manual.

5. When it is done cooking, allow the pressure to release naturally.

6. Carefully remove the rack and dish from the Instant Pot and serve.

Calories: 383

Fat: 10 g

Saturated Fat: 1.3 g

Carbohydrates: 62 g

Fiber: 9 g

Sodium: 197 mg

Protein: 14 g

Cholesterol: 2 mg

Best Steel-Cut Oats

Colleen Heatwole, Burton, MI

Makes 4 servings

Prep. Time: 5 minutes ⚘ *Cooking Time: 3 minutes*

I cup steel-cut oats

2 cups water

I cup unsweetened almond milk

Pinch salt

½ tsp. vanilla extract

I cinnamon stick

¼ cup raisins

¼ cup dried cherries

I tsp. ground cinnamon

¼ cup toasted almonds

Sweetener of choice, *optional*

1. Add all ingredients to the inner pot of the Instant Pot except the toasted almonds and sweetener.

2. Secure the lid and make sure the vent is turned to sealing. Cook 3 minutes on high, using manual function.

3. Let the pressure release naturally.

4. Remove cinnamon stick.

5. Add almonds, and sweetener if desired, and serve.

Tip:

Nondairy milk is best because dairy milk can scorch. Additional milk can be added when eating if desired.

Calories: 276

Fat: 7 g

Saturated Fat: 0.7 g

Carbohydrates: 46 g

Fiber: 7 g

Sodium: 53 mg

Protein: 9 g

Cholesterol: 0 mg

Banana Chocolate Chip Muffins

OVEN

Jen Hoover, Akron, PA
Jane Steiner, Orrville, OH

Makes 24 servings, 1 muffin per serving

Prep. Time: 10 minutes ❧ *Baking Time: 12–20 minutes*

4 large ripe bananas, mashed
6 Tbsp. Splenda Sugar Blend
1 egg
1½ cups whole wheat flour
1 tsp. baking soda
1 tsp. baking powder
5⅓ Tbsp. no-trans-fat tub margarine, melted
½ cup chocolate chips

1. In a good-sized mixing bowl, blend together bananas, Splenda, egg, and flour.

2. Mix in baking soda, baking powder, and melted margarine.

3. Stir in chocolate chips.

4. Bake in lined muffin tins at 375°F for 12–18 minutes, or until toothpick inserted in center comes out clean. Check after 12 minutes to prevent muffins from over-baking.

Tips:

1. Freeze overly ripe bananas with these muffins in mind. Microwave frozen bananas until soft; then follow recipe.
2. You can use ¾ cup whole wheat flour and ¾ cup white flour for these. You can also add 1 Tbsp. wheat germ or flax seed to Step 1.

Calories: 86
Fat: 3 g
Saturated Fat: 1 g
Carbohydrates: 13 g
Fiber: 1 g
Sodium: 100 mg
Protein: 1 g
Cholesterol: 8 mg

OVEN

Morning Maple Muffins

Connie Lynn Miller, Shipshewana, IN

Makes 18 muffins, 1 muffin per serving

Prep. Time: 10 minutes ✿ Baking Time: 15–20 minutes

Muffins:

2 cups whole wheat flour

¼ cup Splenda Brown Sugar Blend

2 tsp. baking powder

½ tsp. salt

¾ cup fat-free milk

½ cup no-trans-fat tub margarine, melted

¼ cup maple syrup

¼ cup fat-free sour cream

I egg

½ tsp. vanilla extract

Topping:

3 Tbsp. flour

3 Tbsp. sugar

2 Tbsp. chopped pecans

½ tsp. cinnamon

2 Tbsp. no-trans-fat tub margarine

1. To make muffins, combine flour, brown sugar blend, baking powder, and salt in a large bowl.

2. In another bowl, combine milk, melted margarine, maple syrup, sour cream, egg, and vanilla.

3. Stir wet ingredients into dry ingredients just until moistened.

4. Fill greased or paper-lined muffin cups ⅔ full.

5. For topping, combine flour, sugar, nuts, and cinnamon.

6. Cut in margarine, using a pastry cutter or two knives, until crumbly.

7. Sprinkle over batter in muffin cups.

8. Bake at 400°F for 15–20 minutes, or until a toothpick inserted near the center comes out clean.

9. Cool 5 minutes before removing from pans to wire racks. Serve warm.

Calories: 154

Fat: 7 g

Saturated Fat: I g

Carbohydrates: 20 g

Fiber: 1.5 g

Sodium: 182 mg

Protein: 3 g

Cholesterol: 11 mg

Pineapple Carrot Muffins

Christie Detamore-Hunsberger, Harrisonburg, VA

Makes 12 servings

Prep. Time: 15 minutes   Baking Time: 15 minutes

1 cup fine, or coarse, dry oat bran

¼ cup whole wheat flour

2 tsp. baking powder

½ tsp. baking soda

1 tsp. cinnamon

1 cup low-fat buttermilk

⅓ cup sugar-free honey

2 Tbsp. unsweetened applesauce

8-oz. can crushed pineapple, packed in water, drained

1 medium carrot, shredded

½ cup raisins

1. Mix first 5 dry ingredients together in a large bowl.

2. Mix remaining ingredients.

3. Mix fruit mixture into dry ingredients until just combined.

4. Fill nonstick muffin tins ⅔ full.

5. Bake at 375°F for 15 minutes, or until toothpick inserted in centers of muffins comes out clean.

Calories: 98
Fat: 1 g
Saturated Fat: 0 g
Carbohydrates: 25 g
Fiber: 2 g
Sodium: 101 mg
Protein: 3 g
Cholesterol: 1 mg

Whole Wheat Pumpkin Muffins

OVEN

Sylvia Beiler, Lowville, NY

Makes 24 servings

Prep. Time: 15 minutes ⚬ *Baking Time: 15 minutes*

1 cup sugar

⅓ cup canola oil

Egg substitute equivalent to 3 eggs, or
6 egg whites

1½ cups pumpkin puree

½ cup water

3 cups whole wheat pastry flour

1½ tsp. baking powder

1 tsp. baking soda

¾ tsp. ground cloves

1 tsp. ground cinnamon

1 tsp. ground nutmeg

1 cup raisins

½ cup chopped walnuts

1. Preheat oven to 400°F.

2. In a large mixer bowl combine sugar, oil, egg substitute, pumpkin puree, and water.

3. In a separate bowl, mix the flour, baking powder, baking soda, and spices.

4. Add dry ingredients to first mixture. Blend with electric mixer.

5. Stir in raisins and walnuts by hand.

6. Spoon mixture into 24 lightly greased muffin cups.

7. Bake 15 minutes, or until tester inserted in centers of muffins comes out clean.

Calories: 152

Fat: 5 g

Saturated Fat: 0.5 g

Carbohydrates: 26 g

Fiber: 2.5 g

Sodium: 60 mg

Protein: 3 g

Cholesterol: 0 mg

Oatmeal Waffles

Deborah Heatwole, Waynesboro, GA

Makes 6 servings

Prep. Time: 5–10 minutes & Cooking Time: 3–5 minutes

1 cup whole wheat pastry flour

⅔ cup uncooked rolled, or quick, oats

⅓ cup cornmeal

2 tsp. baking powder

¼ tsp. baking soda

2 cups skim milk

1 Tbsp. canola oil

Egg substitute equivalent to 2 eggs, or 4 egg whites, beaten

1. Combine dry ingredients in mixing bowl.

2. Stir in milk, oil, and beaten egg substitute or whites.

3. When batter is well blended, cook in waffle iron according to appliance instructions.

Calories: 192

Fat: 4 g

Saturated Fat: 0 g

Carbohydrates: 32 g

Fiber: 4 g

Sodium: 108 mg

Protein: 8 g

Cholesterol: 2 mg

Multigrain Pancakes

Deborah Heatwole, Waynesboro, GA

Makes 6 servings

Prep. Time: 5–10 minutes   *Cooking Time: 10–15 minutes*

1 cup whole wheat pastry flour

½ cup all-purpose flour

¼ cup cornmeal

¼ cup buckwheat flour

2 tsp. baking powder

¼ tsp. baking soda

Egg substitute equivalent to 2 eggs, or 4 egg whites

1 Tbsp. canola oil

2 cups skim milk

1. In a good-sized bowl, mix the dry ingredients thoroughly.

2. Add egg substitute or whites, oil, and milk. Stir well to combine.

3. Cook by ¼ cupfuls on a nonstick or cast-iron skillet sprayed with nonstick cooking spray.

4. When bubbles begin to form on pancakes, flip and brown other side.

5. Serve with maple syrup, honey, or your choice of toppings (not included in analyses).

Calories: 195

Fat: 3 g

Saturated Fat: 0 g

Carbohydrates: 35 g

Fiber: 4 g

Sodium: 110 mg

Protein: 8 g

Cholesterol: 2 mg

Blueberry Wheat Pancakes

Anne Nolt, Thompsontown, PA

Makes 6 servings

Prep. Time: 10 minutes ❧ Cooking Time: 15–20 minutes

1 cup whole wheat pastry flour

½ cup wheat germ

1 Tbsp. Splenda Zero Calorie Granulated Sweetener

2 tsp. baking powder

¼ tsp. baking soda

¾ cup freshly squeezed orange juice (approx. 3 oranges)

¾ cup plain nonfat sugar-free yogurt

2 Tbsp. canola oil

1 large egg, or 2 egg whites

2 cups blueberries

1. In medium bowl, combine dry ingredients. Mix well.

2. In small bowl, combine orange juice, yogurt, oil, and egg. Blend well.

3. Add liquid ingredients to dry ingredients.

4. Add 2 cups blueberries.

5. Stir everything together gently, just until dry ingredients are moistened.

6. Pour batter by ¼ cupfuls onto hot, lightly greased griddle or into large skillet.

7. Turn when bubbles form on top.

8. Cook until second side is golden brown. Continue this process until all the batter is cooked.

9. Serve and enjoy.

Calories: 209

Fat: 7 g

Saturated Fat: 1 g

Carbohydrates: 29 g

Fiber: 4 g

Sodium: 77 mg

Protein: 10 g

Cholesterol: 32 mg

Pumpkin & Ginger Pancakes

Christie Detamore-Hunsberger, Harrisonburg, VA

Makes 12 pancakes, 2 pancakes per serving

Prep. Time: 10 minutes ⚘ *Cooking Time: 15–20 minutes*

I cup whole wheat pastry flour
I tsp. baking powder
½ tsp. baking soda
½ tsp. cinnamon
½ tsp. ground ginger
½ tsp. nutmeg
¾ cup pumpkin
¾ cup skim milk
½ cup plain nonfat sugar-free yogurt
2 Tbsp. oil
I large egg, beaten

1. In a mixing bowl, combine 6 dry ingredients.

2. Stir in 5 wet ingredients.

3. When well combined, drop by ¼ cupfuls onto griddle or into skillet.

4. Cook until bubbles form on top.

5. Flip. Cook until second side is golden brown.

Calories: 77
Fat: 3 g
Saturated Fat: 0 g
Carbohydrates: 10 g
Fiber: 2 g
Sodium: 70 mg
Protein: 4 g
Cholesterol: 16 mg

Berry Breakfast Parfait

NO-COOK

Susan Tjon, Austin, TX

Makes 4 servings

Prep. Time: 15 minutes

2 cups sugar-free low-fat vanilla yogurt
¼ tsp. ground cinnamon
I cup sliced strawberries
½ cup blueberries
½ cup raspberries
I cup low-sugar granola

1. Combine yogurt and cinnamon in small bowl.

2. Combine fruit in medium bowl.

3. For each parfait, layer ¼ cup fruit mixture, then 2 Tbsp. granola, followed by ¼ cup yogurt mixture in parfait glass (or whatever container you choose).

4. Repeat layers once more and top with a sprinkling of granola.

Calories: 355
Fat: 6 g
Saturated Fat: 2 g
Carbohydrates: 68 g
Fiber: 6 g
Sodium: 248 mg
Protein: I I g
Cholesterol: 6 mg

Soups & Chilies

Chicken Vegetable Soup

Maria Shevlin, Sicklerville, NJ

Makes 6 servings

Prep. Time: 12–25 minutes ⚬ *Cooking Time: 4 minutes*

1–2 raw chicken breasts, cubed
½ medium onion, chopped
4 cloves garlic, minced
½ sweet potato, small cubes
1 large carrot, peeled and cubed
4 stalks celery, chopped, leaves included
½ cup frozen corn
¼ cup frozen peas
¼ cup frozen lima beans
1 cup frozen green beans (bite sized)
¼–½ cup chopped savoy cabbage
14½-oz. can low-sodium petite diced tomatoes
3 cups low-sodium chicken bone broth
½ tsp. black pepper
1 tsp. garlic powder
¼ cup chopped fresh parsley
¼–½ tsp. red pepper flakes

1. Add all the ingredients, in the order listed, to the inner pot of the Instant Pot.

2. Lock the lid in place, set the vent to sealing, and press Manual, and cook at high pressure for 4 minutes.

3. Release the pressure manually as soon as cooking time is finished.

Calories: 176
Fat: 3 g
Saturated Fat: 0.6 g
Carbohydrates: 18 g
Fiber: 4 g
Sodium: 169 mg
Protein: 21 g
Cholesterol: 56 mg

STOVETOP

Chicken Spinach Soup

Carna Reitz, Remington, VA

Makes 4–6 servings

Prep. Time: 5 minutes ⚮ *Cooking Time: 20 minutes*

6½ cups low-sodium chicken broth,
divided

2 cups cooked, chopped,
or shredded chicken

1–2 cups frozen chopped spinach

Salt and pepper to taste

2½ Tbsp. arrowroot

1. Put 6 cups broth, chicken, spinach, and salt and pepper in a large stockpot. Bring to a boil.

2. Meanwhile, mix arrowroot and remaining ½ cup broth together in a jar. Put on lid and shake until smooth. When soup is boiling, slowly pour into soup to thicken, stirring constantly.

3. Continue stirring and cooking until soup thickens.

Calories: 116

Fat: 2 g

Saturated Fat: 0.5 g

Carbohydrates: 3 g

Fiber: 1.5 g

Sodium: 182 mg

Protein: 21 g

Cholesterol: 40 mg

Egg Drop Chicken Soup

Kathryn Yoder, Minot, ND

Makes 6 servings

Prep. Time: 10 minutes   Cooking Time: 12–15 minutes

4½ cups water

4 low-sodium chicken bouillon cubes

4 oz. cooked chicken, shredded

½ cup finely shredded carrot

1 tsp. finely chopped fresh parsley, or
½ tsp. dried parsley

1 tsp. low-sodium soy sauce

2 egg whites, lightly beaten

4 tsp. sliced green onions

1. In large saucepan, dissolve bouillon cubes in water over medium heat.

2. Add shredded chicken, carrot, parsley, and soy sauce.

3. Bring to a boil, stirring occasionally. Continue boiling, 4–5 minutes.

4. Slowly dribble lightly beaten egg whites into boiling soup, stirring constantly until the egg has cooked.

5. Serve with scallions as garnish.

Calories: 53

Fat: 1 g

Saturated Fat: 0 g

Carbohydrates: 0 g

Fiber: 0 g

Sodium: 380 mg

Protein: 11 g

Cholesterol: 16 mg

Bean Soup with Turkey Sausage

Dorothy Reise, Severna Park, MD
D. Fern Ruth, Chalfont, PA

Makes 4 servings

Prep. Time: 10 minutes ❧ Cooking Time: 15–20 minutes

8 oz. turkey kielbasa

4 cups low-sodium chicken broth

2 (15-oz.) cans cannellini beans, rinsed and drained

½–1 cup chopped onion

2 tsp. fresh minced basil

¼ tsp. coarsely ground pepper

1 clove garlic, minced

1 carrot, peeled and sliced, or 1 cup baby carrots

½ red, yellow, or orange bell pepper, sliced

3 cups fresh spinach, cleaned

¼ cup fresh chopped parsley

1. Cut turkey kielbasa lengthwise, and then into ½-inch slices. Sauté in Dutch oven or large saucepan until browned, stirring occasionally so it doesn't stick.

2. Combine all ingredients in pan except spinach and parsley.

3. Bring to boil, and then reduce heat. Cover and simmer 10–15 minutes, or until onion and carrots are tender.

4. Remove stems from fresh spinach, stack, and cut into 1-inch strips. Remove soup from heat and stir in spinach and parsley until spinach wilts.

5. Serve immediately.

Variation:

For a thicker soup, remove 1 cup of hot soup after Step 3 and carefully process in firmly covered blender or food processor until smooth. Stir back into soup and continue with Step 4.

Calories: 389

Fat: 6 g

Saturated Fat: 2 g

Carbohydrates: 54 g

Fiber: 12 g

Sodium: 1415 mg

Protein: 29 g

Cholesterol: 30 mg

Buffalo Chicken Veggie Chili

Maria Shevlin, Sicklerville, NJ

Makes 4 servings

Prep. Time: 10 minutes   Cooking Time: 20 minutes

1–2 lb. ground white meat chicken

1 Tbsp. olive oil

¼ cup thin-sliced carrots

¼ cup green beans, cut into small pieces

4 large mushrooms, chopped

½ cup onion, chopped fine

2–3 cloves garlic, minced

1 cup low-sodium tomato sauce

¼ cup hot sauce

Salt and pepper to taste, if needed

1 Tbsp. reduced-sodium fajita seasoning

1. Brown the meat; remove from pan and cover to keep warm.

2. Heat olive oil in a pot, then add the carrots, green beans, mushrooms, onion, and garlic. Sauté until al dente.

3. Add the meat into the pot with all the remaining ingredients and mix well.

4. Simmer, covered, for approximately 5–10 minutes.

5. Serve and enjoy.

Serving suggestion:
Feel free to top with green onion and sour cream if desired.

Calories: 428

Fat: 22 g

Saturated Fat: 6 g

Carbohydrates: 12 g

Fiber: 1 g

Sodium: 688 mg

Protein: 42 g

Cholesterol: 195 mg

Broccoli Rabe & Sausage Soup

STOVETOP

Carlene Horne, Bedford, NH

Makes 5 servings

Prep. Time: 15 minutes ⚬ *Cooking Time: 15 minutes*

1 Tbsp. olive oil

1 onion, chopped

½ lb. lean fresh Italian turkey sausage, casing removed, sliced

5 cups chopped broccoli rabe, about 1 bunch

32-oz. carton no-salt-added chicken broth

1 cup water

8 oz. frozen tortellini

1. Heat olive oil in a soup pot.

2. Add onion and sausage and sauté until tender.

3. Add broccoli rabe and sauté a few more minutes.

4. Pour broth and water into pan; bring to simmer.

5. Add tortellini and cook a few minutes until tender.

Variation:

Substitute any green such as Swiss chard, kale, or spinach for the broccoli rabe.

Calories: 258
Fat: 15 g
Saturated Fat: 3 g
Carbohydrates: 8 g
Fiber: 3 g
Sodium: 898 mg
Protein: 23 g
Cholesterol: 71 mg

Turkey & Black Bean Chili

STOVETOP

Eileen B. Jarvis, Saint Augustine, FL

Makes 8 servings

Prep. Time: 10 minutes   Cooking Time: 15–20 minutes

1 lb. lean ground turkey

2 (15-oz.) cans no-salt-added black beans, rinsed and drained, *divided*

½ cup water

1 cup medium, or hot, chunky salsa

2 (8-oz.) cans no-salt-added tomato sauce

1 Tbsp. chili powder

Low-fat sour cream, *optional*

1. Brown meat in large saucepan over medium-high heat. Drain off drippings.

2. While meat cooks, mash a can black beans.

3. Add mashed beans, second can of rinsed and drained beans, water, salsa, tomato sauce, and seasoning into saucepan. Stir well.

4. Cover. Cook over medium heat 10 minutes. Stir occasionally.

5. If you wish, top individual servings with sour cream and/or reduced-fat cheese.

Calories: 249
Fat: 5 g
Saturated Fat: 1 g
Carbohydrates: 31 g
Fiber: 11 g
Sodium: 558 mg
Protein: 22 g
Cholesterol: 39 mg

INSTANT POT

Turkey Chili

Reita F. Yoder, Carlsbad, NM

Makes 8 servings

Prep. Time: 20 minutes ⚘ *Cooking Time: 5 minutes*

2 lb. ground turkey

1 small onion, chopped

1 garlic clove, minced

16-oz. can low-sodium pinto, or kidney, beans

2 cups chopped fresh tomatoes

2 cups no-salt-added tomato sauce

16-oz. can Ro-Tel Diced Tomatoes and Green Chilies

1-oz. package low-sodium chili seasoning

1. Crumble ground turkey in the inner pot and brown on the Sauté setting until cooked. Add in onion and garlic and sauté an additional 5 minutes, stirring constantly.

2. Add remaining ingredients to inner pot and mix well.

3. Secure the lid and make sure the vent is set to sealing. Cook on Manual for 5 minutes.

4. When cook time is up, let the pressure release naturally for 10 minutes, then manually release the rest.

Calories: 245

Fat: 2 g

Saturated Fat: 0.5 g

Carbohydrates: 24 g

Fiber: 5 g

Sodium: 492 mg

Protein: 34 g

Cholesterol: 55 mg

Black Bean & Mushroom Chili

STOVETOP

Maria Shevlin, Sicklerville, NJ

Makes 4–6 servings

Prep. Time: 5 minutes ⚬ Cooking Time: 25 minutes

2 tsp. olive oil

4 cloves garlic, minced

1 large onion, diced

8-oz. pkg. mushrooms, chopped

15-oz. can low-sodium black beans, rinsed and drained

2 (14½-oz.) cans low-sodium petite diced tomatoes

1 can water

1 low-sodium vegetable bouillon cube

1 tsp. cumin

1 Tbsp. garlic powder

1 Tbsp. onion powder

1 Tbsp. parsley flakes

2 tsp. paprika

1. In a large stock pot, add olive oil, garlic, and onion. Cook until softened (about 5 minutes) over medium heat. Stir often.

2. Add the mushrooms, stir, and cover. Cook for an additional 3–4 minutes.

3. Remove cover and add the remaining ingredients including all of the spices. Cover and simmer on low for an additional 15 minutes.

Serving suggestions:

Serve with any or all of the following:

Steamed organic brown rice

Green onion

Plain nonfat Greek yogurt or nonfat sour cream

Reduced-fat shredded sharp cheese

Calories: 178

Fat: 2 g

Saturated Fat: 0 g

Carbohydrates: 30 g

Fiber: 8 g

Sodium: 249 mg

Protein: 10 g

Cholesterol: 0 mg

Black Bean Soup with Onion, Cilantro & Lime Salsa

Melanie Mohler, Ephrata, PA

Makes 6 servings

Prep. Time: 15 minutes ❧ Cooking Time: 15 minutes

4 cups low-sodium canned black beans, rinsed and drained

1 Tbsp. minced fresh garlic

1½ cups low-sodium, fat-free chicken broth, *divided*

¼–½ tsp. dried thyme, according to your taste preference

3 Tbsp. fat-free sour cream

Salsa Ingredients:

⅓ cup fresh cilantro, washed and stemmed

½ onion, coarsely chopped

Juice of ½ lime, or 1 Tbsp. bottled lime juice

1. Puree black beans and garlic in blender or food processor, adding chicken broth as needed to help with blending.

2. Pour puree into saucepan. Add remaining chicken broth and thyme.

3. Cover and simmer over low heat, about 15 minutes.

4. While soup is simmering, puree cilantro, onion, and lime juice in processor until smooth. Place in small bowl.

5. Place sour cream in another small bowl.

6. Serve salsa and sour cream with soup, to be spooned on top of each serving.

Calories: 170

Fat: 1 g

Saturated Fat: 0 g

Carbohydrates: 30 g

Fiber: 10 g

Sodium: 39 mg

Protein: 12 g

Cholesterol: 1 mg

Low-Fat Broccoli Soup

Carolyn Snader, Ephrata, PA
Joyce Nolt, Richland, PA

Makes 4 servings

Prep. Time: 10–15 minutes ❧ *Cooking Time: 12 minutes*

1 lb. (about 5 cups) chopped fresh, or frozen, broccoli
½ cup chopped onion
14½-oz. can low-sodium, fat-free chicken, or vegetable, broth
2 Tbsp. arrowroot
12-oz. can evaporated skim milk
½ cup grated low-fat cheddar cheese

1. In a good-sized stockpot, cook broccoli and onion in chicken broth, 5–10 minutes.

2. Carefully puree half of mixture in blender.

3. Stir back into remaining broccoli in stockpot.

4. Place arrowroot in jar with tight-fitting lid. Pour in a little milk. Cover and shake until smooth.

5. Pour rest of milk into jar. Cover and shake until smooth. Stir into soup.

6. Cover and simmer 2 minutes.

7. Top each serving with 2 Tbsp. grated cheese.

Calories: 175
Fat: 2 g
Saturated Fat: 1 g
Carbohydrates: 19 g
Fiber: 3 g
Sodium: 323 mg
Protein: 16 g
Cholesterol: 7 mg

Flavorful Tomato Soup

Shari Ladd, Hudson, MI

Makes 4 servings

Prep. Time: 10 minutes   *Cooking Time: 20 minutes*

2 Tbsp. chopped onions

1 Tbsp. extra-virgin olive oil

3 Tbsp. whole wheat flour

2 tsp. sugar

½ tsp. pepper

¼ tsp. dried basil

½ tsp. dried oregano

¼ tsp. dried thyme

1 qt. stewed tomatoes, no salt added, undrained

2 cups skim milk

1. Sauté onion in oil in stockpot.

2. Stir in flour and seasonings.

3. Stir in stewed tomatoes, stirring constantly. Bring to a boil and boil 1 minute.

4. Add 2 cups milk. If soup is too thick, add a little water. Stir well.

5. Simmer 10 minutes but do not boil.

Calories: 182

Fat: 6 g

Saturated Fat: 1 g

Carbohydrates: 26 g

Fiber: 3 g

Sodium: 1592 mg

Protein: 7 g

Cholesterol: 2 mg

Veggie Minestrone

Dorothy VanDeest, Memphis, TN

Makes 8 servings

Prep. Time: 15 minutes   *Cooking Time: 4 minutes*

2 Tbsp. olive oil

I large onion, chopped

I clove garlic, minced

4 cups low-sodium chicken or vegetable stock

16-oz. can low-sodium kidney beans, rinsed and drained

14½-oz. can no-salt-added diced tomatoes

2 medium carrots, sliced thin

¼ tsp. dried oregano

¼ tsp. pepper

½ cup whole wheat elbow macaroni, uncooked

4 oz. fresh spinach

½ cup grated Parmesan cheese

1. Set the Instant Pot to the Sauté function and heat the olive oil.

2. When the olive oil is heated, add the onion and garlic to the inner pot and sauté for 5 minutes.

3. Press Cancel and add the stock, kidney beans, tomatoes, carrots, oregano, and pepper. Gently pour in the macaroni, but *do not stir*. Just push the noodles gently under the liquid.

4. Secure the lid and set the vent to sealing.

5. Manually set the cook time for 4 minutes on high pressure.

6. When the cooking time is over, manually release the pressure and remove the lid when the pin drops.

7. Stir in the spinach and let wilt a few minutes.

8. Sprinkle 1 Tbsp. grated Parmesan on each individual bowl of this soup. Enjoy!

Calories: 187

Fat: 5 g

Saturated Fat: I g

Carbohydrates: 25 g

Fiber: 6 g

Sodium: 166 mg

Protein: I I g

Cholesterol: 4 mg

Main Dishes

Chicken

Lemon Grilled Chicken Breasts

Wilma Haberkamp, Fairbank, IA

GRILL

Makes 4 servings

Prep. Time: 15 minutes 🔪 Grilling Time: 4–5 minutes

1 ¼ lb. boneless, skinless
chicken breasts

2 lemons

2 Tbsp. olive oil

½ tsp. salt

½ tsp. coarsely ground pepper

1. Prepare grill for direct grilling over medium heat.

2. Pound chicken to uniform ¼-inch thickness.

3. Grate 1½ Tbsp. lemon peel and squeeze 3 Tbsp. lemon juice into a small bowl.

4. Add oil, salt, and pepper. Whisk until well blended.

5. In large bowl, toss chicken with marinade.

6. Place chicken on grill. Cook 2–2½ minutes.

7. Turn over. Cook 2–2½ minutes more, or until juices run clear.

Serving suggestion:
This would go well with Zucchini Ribbons on page 171 or Italian-Style Broccoli on page 177.

Calories: 241

Fat: 11 g

Saturated Fat: 2 g

Carbohydrates: 6 g

Fiber: 3 g

Sodium: 306 mg

Protein: 33 g

Cholesterol: 103 mg

Buttery Lemon Chicken

Judy Gascho, Woodburn, OR

Makes 4 servings

Prep. Time: 15 minutes ☙ Cooking Time: 7 minutes

2 Tbsp. margarine

I medium onion, chopped

4 cloves garlic, minced

½ tsp. paprika

½ tsp. pepper

I tsp. dried parsley, or I Tbsp. chopped fresh parsley

2 lb. boneless chicken breasts or thighs

½ cup low-sodium chicken broth

⅓ cup lemon juice

I tsp. salt

1–2 Tbsp. arrowroot

I Tbsp. water

1. Set the Instant Pot to Sauté. When it is hot, add margarine to the inner pot and melt.

2. Add the onion, garlic, paprika, pepper, and parsley to melted margarine and sauté until onion starts to soften. Push onion to side of pot.

3. With the Instant Pot still at sauté, add the chicken and sear on each side 3–5 minutes.

4. Mix broth, lemon juice, and salt together. Pour over chicken and stir to mix all together.

5. Put on lid and set Instant Pot, move vent to sealing and press Poultry. Set cook time for 7 minutes. Let depressurize naturally.

6. Remove chicken, leaving sauce in pot. Mix arrowroot in water and add to sauce. (Can start with 1 Tbsp., and use second one if sauce isn't thick enough.)

Serving suggestion:

Serve chicken and sauce over whole wheat noodles or brown rice.

Calories: 350

Fat: 12 g

Saturated Fat: 2 g

Carbohydrates: 7 g

Fiber: I g

Sodium: 658 mg

Protein: 52 g

Cholesterol: 166 mg

French Onion Chicken

INSTANT POT

Mary Seielstad, Sparks, NV

Makes 6 servings

Prep. Time: 10 minutes   Cooking Time: 12 minutes

2 lb. chicken breasts, trimmed of skin and fat

10¾-oz. can 98% fat-free, reduced-sodium cream of mushroom soup

12 oz. water

1 pkg. reduced-sodium French onion soup mix

1 cup low-sodium chicken broth

1. Place the chicken into the Instant Pot.

2. Combine soup, water, French onion soup mix and chicken broth. Pour over chicken.

3. Secure the lid and make sure vent is set to sealing. Cook on Manual mode for 12 minutes.

4. When cook time is up, let the pressure release naturally for 5 minutes and then release the rest manually.

Serving suggestion:

This would go well with Almond Rice on page 190 or Garlic Mushrooms on page 178.

Calories: 213
Fat: 5 g
Saturated Fat: 1 g
Carbohydrates: 4 g
Fiber: 1 g
Sodium: 452 mg
Protein: 36 g
Cholesterol: 112 mg

Italian Chicken & Broccoli

Liz Clapper, Lancaster, PA

Makes 6 servings

Prep. Time: 15 minutes ♨ Cooking Time: 15 minutes

2 cups uncooked whole-grain macaroni

1 lb. boneless, skinless chicken tenderloins

1 Tbsp. olive oil

4 medium carrots, sliced thin

2 cloves garlic, finely chopped

1 head broccoli, chopped into florets (about 4 cups)

½ cup low-fat, low-sodium chicken broth

1½ Tbsp. Italian seasoning, unsalted, like Mrs. Dash

¼ cup Parmesan shredded cheese

1. Cook pasta according to package directions until al dente.

2. Meanwhile, in a large skillet or saucepan, cook chicken in olive oil about 7 minutes, or until cooked through.

3. Remove chicken from pan and keep warm.

4. Add sliced carrots to same pan. Sauté 2 minutes.

5. Add garlic and broccoli to carrots. Sauté 2 minutes.

6. Add broth and Italian seasoning. Heat until broth simmers.

7. Cut chicken into bite-sized pieces. Stir into skillet with vegetables and cook 3 more minutes.

8. Toss with cooked pasta. Sprinkle with Parmesan and serve immediately.

Calories: 309

Fat: 9 g

Saturated Fat: 2 g

Carbohydrates: 25 g

Fiber: 4 g

Sodium: 337 mg

Protein: 34 g

Cholesterol: 76 mg

OVEN

Encore Dijon Chicken

Dorothy VanDeest, Memphis, TN

Makes 6 servings, 1 breast half per serving

Prep. Time: 5–10 minutes   *Baking Time: 20 minutes*

½ tsp. Italian seasoning

4 Tbsp. Dijon mustard

2 Tbsp. olive oil

1 tsp. garlic powder, or refrigerated minced garlic

6 boneless chicken breast halves, about 6 oz. each in weight

1. Grease a 9 × 13-inch baking dish.

2. Mix Italian seasoning, mustard, oil, and garlic in either a large bowl or plastic bag.

3. Add chicken pieces, one at a time. Dredge or shake to coat each piece.

4. Lay in baking dish.

5. Bake at 375°F for 20 minutes, or until thermometer inserted in center of each piece registers 165°F.

Serving suggestion:

This would go well with Roasted Asparagus on page 180 or Sautéed Cabbage on page 186.

Calories: 324

Fat: 11 g

Saturated Fat: 2 g

Carbohydrates: 0 g

Fiber: 0 g

Sodium: 336 mg

Protein: 53 g

Cholesterol: 172 mg

Chicken Curry

Tina Hartman, Lancaster, PA

Makes 8 servings, about 3–4 oz. per serving

Prep. Time: 20 minutes ⚮ Cooking Time: 10–15 minutes

3 Tbsp. no-trans-fat tub margarine

¼ cup minced onion

1½ tsp. curry powder

3 Tbsp. whole wheat flour

¾ tsp. salt

¾ tsp. Splenda Stevia Granulated Sugar

⅛ tsp. ground ginger

1 cup lower-sodium, fat-free chicken broth

1 cup fat-free milk

2 cups diced, cooked chicken

½ tsp. lemon juice

1. In good-sized skillet, melt margarine over low heat.

2. Sauté onion and curry in margarine.

3. Blend in flour and seasonings.

4. Cook over low heat until mixture is smooth and bubbly. (This removes the raw flour taste.)

5. Remove from heat.

6. Stir in chicken broth and milk.

7. Return to heat. Bring to a boil, stirring constantly.

8. Boil one more minute, continuing to stir.

9. Remove from heat. Stir in chicken and lemon juice.

10. Serve over cooked rice, and with toppings for individuals to choose.

Calories: 125

Fat: 6 g

Saturated Fat: 1 g

Carbohydrates: 5 g

Fiber: 1 g

Sodium: 281 mg

Protein: 13 g

Cholesterol: 30 mg

Jerk-Seasoned Chicken & Pepper Sauté

STOVETOP

Louise Bodziony, Sunrise Beach, MO

Makes 4 servings

Prep. Time: 5–10 minutes ⚬ Cooking Time: 15–20 minutes

1 lb. boneless, skinless chicken breast
halves, cut into ¾-inch-wide strips

2 tsp. Caribbean jerk seasoning

1 pkg. frozen bell pepper
and onion stir-fry

⅓ cup freshly squeezed orange juice
(approx. 1 orange squeezed)

2 tsp. arrowroot

1. Spray large nonstick skillet lightly with cooking spray. Heat over medium heat until hot.

2. Add chicken and jerk seasoning. Cook and stir 5–7 minutes, or until chicken is no longer pink.

3. Add pepper and onion stir-fry. Cover and cook 3–5 minutes, or until vegetables are crisp-tender. Stir occasionally.

4. Meanwhile, in a small bowl, combine orange juice and arrowroot. Blend until smooth. Add to mixture in skillet; cook and stir until bubbly and thickened.

Serving suggestion:
This is good served over cooked brown rice.

Calories: 162
Fat: 3 g
Saturated Fat: 1 g
Carbohydrates: 7 g
Fiber: 1 g
Sodium: 54 mg
Protein: 26 g
Cholesterol: 83 mg

Honey-Chicken Stir Fry

Anya Kauffman, Sheldon, WI

Makes 6 servings

Prep. Time: 15 minutes ⚘ *Cooking Time: 10 minutes*

1 lb. boneless, skinless chicken breast

2 Tbsp. olive oil, *divided*

4 cups sliced raw vegetables (your choice of a combination of cabbage, onion, celery, carrots, broccoli, cauliflower, and sweet peppers)

Sauce:

1½ cups freshly squeezed orange juice (approx. 3 oranges, squeezed)

⅔ cup sugar-free honey

1 Tbsp. low-sodium soy sauce

2 Tbsp. arrowroot

½ tsp. ground ginger

1. Slice chicken breast into thin strips. Set aside.

2. Combine sauce ingredients in a bowl.

3. In a large skillet, stir-fry meat in 1 Tbsp. oil until no longer pink. Remove from skillet and set aside.

4. In remaining oil and in same skillet, stir-fry vegetables on high heat until crisp-tender.

5. Stir in meat and sauce until sauce is somewhat thickened.

Serving suggestion:
Serve over hot brown rice if you choose.

Calories: 286

Fat: 7 g

Saturated Fat: 1 g

Carbohydrates: 40 g

Fiber: 1 g

Sodium: 153 mg

Protein: 19 g

Cholesterol: 55 mg

Chicken Scampi à la Mamma

Maria Shevlin, Sicklerville, NJ

Makes 4 servings

Prep. Time: 5–8 minutes   *Cooking Time: 20–22 minutes*

6 cups water

8 oz. uncooked whole wheat spaghetti

2 Tbsp. margarine

1 Tbsp. olive oil

3 Tbsp. garlic, chopped fine

2 red bell peppers, cut into thin strips

1 low-sodium vegetable bouillon cube
dissolved in 1 cup hot water

¼ cup low-sodium chicken stock

2 tsp. Italian seasoning

½ tsp. black pepper

1 tsp. garlic powder

1 medium onion, cut into thin strips

2–3 chicken breasts, cut thin,
and into small pieces

1. Start water to boil in a pan. While waiting for it to come to a boil, continue on with the remaining directions. When the water does boil, cook the pasta according to the directions on the box.

2. Add margarine, oil, and chopped garlic to large pan. Cook approximately 3 minutes.

3. Add the remaining ingredients. Simmer, covered, approximately 20–22 minutes, turning the chicken occasionally.

4. Serve over the freshly cooked pasta.

Serving suggestion:

Serve over brown rice instead of pasta if you choose.

Calories: 475

Fat: 15 g

Saturated Fat: 3 g

Carbohydrates: 50 g

Fiber: 7 g

Sodium: 161 mg

Protein: 38 g

Cholesterol: 86 mg

Basil Chicken Strips

Melissa Raber, Millersburg, OH

Makes 2 servings

Prep. Time: 10 minutes   Cooking Time: 10 minutes

½ lb. boneless, skinless chicken breasts, cut into ¾-inch-wide strips

2 Tbsp. whole wheat flour

3 Tbsp. margarine

2 Tbsp. red wine vinegar or cider vinegar

½ tsp. dried basil

1. In a large resealable plastic bag, shake chicken strips and flour until coated.

2. In a large skillet over medium-high heat, melt margarine. Add chicken. Sauté for 5 minutes.

3. Stir in the vinegar and basil. Cook until chicken juices run clear.

Serving suggestion:

This would go well with Almond Rice on page 190 or Tangy Green Beans on page 170.

Calories: 317

Fat: 20 g

Saturated Fat: 4 g

Carbohydrates: 6 g

Fiber: 1 g

Sodium: 252 mg

Protein: 27 g

Cholesterol: 83 mg

Chicken & Quinoa Veggie Bowl

Hope Comerford, Clinton Township, MI

Makes 4 servings

Prep. Time: 10 minutes ❧ *Baking Time: 15 minutes*

½ cup quinoa

3 bunches broccolini

2 cups cherry tomatoes

½ cup sliced red onion

¼ cup olive oil, *divided*

Salt and pepper to taste

2 cups chopped rotisserie chicken meat

2 avocados, sliced, *divided*

1. Begin the quinoa and cook according to the package directions. Meanwhile, proceed with the following steps.

2. Preheat the oven to 375°F.

3. Trim 2 inches off the ends of the broccolini.

4. Between 2 baking sheets, spread out the broccolini. Arrange the cherry tomatoes and red onion around and between the broccolini.

5. Drizzle each pan of vegetables with 2 Tbsp. olive oil. Sprinkle each with the desired amount of salt and pepper.

6. Place in oven and bake for 15 minutes.

7. Divide the quinoa evenly between 4 bowls. Divide the chicken evenly between the 4 bowls.

8. When the vegetables are done, divide the vegetables evenly between the 4 bowls.

9. Top each bowl with ½ of a sliced avocado.

10. Eat and enjoy!

Calories: 418

Fat: 28 g

Saturated Fat: 4 g

Carbohydrates: 19 g

Fiber: 8 g

Sodium: 84 mg

Protein: 27 g

Cholesterol: 60 mg

Firecracker Ground Chicken & Green Beans

Maria Shevlin, Sicklerville, NJ

Makes 4 servings

Prep. Time: 5 minutes & Cooking Time: 15 minutes

4 cups frozen green beans, thawed

I cup water

I Tbsp. avocado oil

2 lb. ground chicken, turkey, or beef

2–3 Tbsp. dried onion flakes

2–3 tsp. paprika (not smoked)

I tsp. onion powder

I tsp. garlic powder

½ tsp. salt

½ tsp. black pepper

1–2 heaping tsp. crushed red pepper flakes (depends on your spice level)

2 Tbsp. Splenda Brown Sugar Blend

¼–½ cup additional water, *optional*

1. In a pot, steam the green beans with the 1 cup of water, then set aside, covered, to keep warm.

2. Meanwhile, in a large fry pan, heat the oil and ground protein of choice. Cook until half done.

3. Add in the seasonings, the green beans, and the brown sugar blend, and continue to cook until the ground protein is done. Add water if desired.

4. Mix well; taste and adjust seasonings.

Serving suggestion:

Serve with avocado if desired and/or over microwaveable steamed rice.

Note:

If you prefer to enjoy this without the spice, just omit the red pepper flakes.

Calories: 445

Fat: 22 g

Saturated Fat: 6 g

Carbohydrates: 20 g

Fiber: 5 g

Sodium: 379 mg

Protein: 43 g

Cholesterol: 195 mg

Egg Roll in a Bowl

STOVETOP

Maria Shevlin, Sicklerville, NJ

Makes 6–8 servings

Prep. Time: 5–8 minutes ⚶ *Cooking Time: 20–22 minutes*

2 tsp. olive oil

1 lb. ground chicken sausage

2 onions, diced

6 cloves garlic, minced

4 stalks celery, diced

1 heaping cup diced bell peppers

2 cups shredded/chopped cabbage, packed

1 cup frozen broccoli, thawed

1 cup frozen cauliflower, thawed

3 eggs, scrambled

4 green onions, chopped

1. Heat the olive oil in a pan and brown the chicken sausage with the onions and garlic.

2. Add in the celery, peppers, cabbage, broccoli, and cauliflower and mix well. Cook an additional 10 minutes.

3. When done cooking, gently fold in the cooked eggs. Top with the green onion.

Calories: 184

Fat: 11 g

Saturated Fat: 3 g

Carbohydrates: 8 g

Fiber: 2 g

Sodium: 480 mg

Protein: 12 g

Cholesterol: 126 mg

Buffalo Chicken Meatballs

Maria Shevlin, Sicklerville, NJ

Makes 2–3 servings

Prep. Time: 5 minutes   Cooking Time: 25 minutes

Meatballs:

I lb. ground chicken or turkey

I Tbsp. minced onion

I tsp. garlic powder

I egg, beaten

I (1.25-oz.) bag of pork rinds, ground
(I use the spicy ones)

Salt and pepper to taste

Sauce:

2 cups low-sodium tomato sauce

¼–½ cup hot sauce

I tsp. garlic powder

½ tsp. salt

½ tsp. black pepper

I Tbsp. parsley flakes

1. Combine all meatball ingredients and roll into approximately 16–18 meatballs.

2. Cook in a nonstick pan, lightly sprayed with nonstick spray. Brown on all sides, then cook about 15 minutes, or until cooked through.

3. Mix the sauce ingredients in a pan. Add to the browned meatballs, cover, and simmer for approximately 10 minutes over low heat. Stir gently.

Calories: 413

Fat: 18 g

Saturated Fat: 5 g

Carbohydrates: 14 g

Fiber: 1 g

Sodium: 1246 mg

Protein: 39 g

Cholesterol: 203 mg

Chicken Fajitas

STOVETOP

Becky Frey, Lebanon, PA

Makes 12 servings

Prep. Time: 20–30 minutes ⚬ Marinating Time: 15 minutes ⚬ Cooking Time: 6–8 minutes

¼ cup lime juice

1–2 cloves garlic, minced

1 tsp. chili powder

½ tsp. ground cumin

3 lb. boneless, skinless chicken breasts, cut into ¼-inch slices

1 large onion, sliced

½ green bell sweet pepper, slivered

½ red bell sweet pepper, slivered

12 whole wheat tortillas, 8-inch in diameter

½ cup salsa

½ cup nonfat sour cream

½ cup your favorite low-fat shredded cheese

1. Combine first four ingredients in a large bowl.

2. Add chicken slices. Stir until chicken is well coated.

3. Marinate for 15 minutes.

4. Cook chicken mixture in large hot nonstick skillet for 3 minutes, or until no longer pink.

5. Stir in onion and peppers. Cook 3–5 minutes, or until done to your liking.

6. Divide mixture evenly among tortillas.

7. Top each with 2 tsp. salsa, 2 tsp. sour cream, and 2 tsp. shredded cheese.

8. Roll up and serve.

Calories: 175

Fat: 3 g

Saturated Fat: 1 g

Carbohydrates: 7 g

Fiber: 2 g

Sodium: 176 mg

Protein: 29 g

Cholesterol: 85 mg

STOVETOP

Soft Chicken Tacos

Natalia Showalter, Mount Solon, VA

Makes 5–6 servings

Prep. Time: 15 minutes   Cooking Time: 15 minutes

I lb. boneless, skinless chicken breasts, cubed

15-oz. can low-sodium black beans, rinsed and drained

I cup low-sodium salsa

I Tbsp. low-sodium taco seasoning

6 whole wheat flour tortillas, warmed

1. In nonstick skillet, cook chicken until juices run clear.

2. Add beans, salsa, and seasoning. Heat through.

3. Spoon chicken mixture down center of each tortilla.

4. Garnish with toppings of your choice.

Calories: 324

Fat: 6 g

Saturated Fat: 3 g

Carbohydrates: 39 g

Fiber: 11 g

Sodium: 592 mg

Protein: 28 g

Cholesterol: 55 mg

Chicken & Broccoli Pita Sandwiches

Vonnie Oyer, Hubbard, OR

Makes 4–6 servings

Prep. Time: 15 minutes

2 cups chopped cooked chicken

2 tomatoes, chopped

1½ cups chopped raw broccoli

1 hard-boiled egg, chopped

⅓ cup cooked brown rice

½ cup grated low-fat cheese

1 avocado, chopped, *optional*

4 whole wheat pita breads

Dressing:

2 Tbsp. sugar-free honey

2 Tbsp. prepared mustard

¾ cup light mayonnaise

1. Mix chicken, tomatoes, broccoli, egg, rice, cheese, and avocado together in a large bowl.

2. Mix dressing ingredients in a small bowl.

3. Pour dressing over chicken mixture and stir gently.

4. Cut pita breads in half. Fill with chicken mixture.

Calories: 404

Fat: 16 g

Saturated Fat: 5 g

Carbohydrates: 41 g

Fiber: 4 g

Sodium: 779 mg

Protein: 25 g

Cholesterol: 94 mg

Turkey

Mild Indian Curry

Vic and Christina Buckwalter, Keezletown, VA

Makes 4–6 servings

Prep. Time: 10 minutes 🌿 *Cooking Time: 15-20 minutes*

2–3 cups uncooked instant brown rice

1 lb. ground turkey

1 onion, chopped

3 cloves garlic, finely chopped

1 Tbsp. freshly grated ginger

2 tsp. coriander

2 tsp. cumin

1 tsp. turmeric

¼ tsp. ground cloves

¼ tsp. cayenne pepper

¾ cup low-sodium tomato sauce

2 tsp. Morton Salt Substitute

2 Tbsp. Splenda Zero Calorie
Granulated Sugar

¼ cup plain nonfat yogurt

Topping options:

Grated low-fat cheese

Chopped fresh onions

Orange sections

Tomatoes

Peanuts

1. Begin by preparing the instant brown rice according to the box directions. Once it is cooking, proceed with the following steps.

2. In a large skillet, brown turkey, onion, and garlic together. Drain off any drippings.

3. Add ginger, coriander, cumin, turmeric, ground cloves, and cayenne pepper to turkey mixture. Cook 1 minute.

4. Stir in tomato sauce, salt substitute, and sugar. Cook 10 minutes.

5. Just before serving, blend in yogurt.

6. Serve over the cooked brown rice.

7. Send small bowls of each topping that you choose around the table after the rice and curry have been passed.

Calories: 228

Fat: 2 g

Saturated Fat: 1 g

Carbohydrates: 29 g

Fiber: 2 g

Sodium: 207 mg

Protein: 22 g

Cholesterol: 38 mg

STOVETOP

Turkey Steaks Dijon

Christie Detamore-Hunsberger, Harrisonburg, VA

Makes 4 servings

Prep. Time: 5 minutes *Cooking Time: 15 minutes*

1 lb. turkey steaks
¼ tsp. black pepper, *optional*
1½ Tbsp. margarine
1 cup low-sodium beef broth
1 Tbsp. arrowroot dissolved in 3 Tbsp. water
1½ Tbsp. Dijon-style mustard
⅓ cup chopped onion, *optional*

1. Sprinkle turkey steaks with pepper if you wish.

2. Heat margarine in skillet.

3. Brown steaks 3 minutes per side. Remove steaks and keep warm. Drain off drippings from skillet.

4. Slowly add broth to hot pan, stirring to dissolve brown particles from bottom of pan. Stir in arrowroot dissolved in water, stirring until thickened. Stir in mustard, and onion if you wish.

5. Reduce heat to medium. Return steaks to skillet and settle into sauce. Tilt pan and spoon sauce over top of steaks.

6. Cover and simmer 2–3 minutes, or just until turkey is done.

7. Place steaks on serving platter, and spoon sauce over before serving.

Serving suggestion:
This would go well with Simple Salted Carrots on page 182 or Broccoli Dijon on page 175.

Calories: 168
Fat: 7 g
Saturated Fat: 1 g
Carbohydrates: 0 g
Fiber: 0 g
Sodium: 391 mg
Protein: 27 g
Cholesterol: 60 mg

Sweet & Sour Sausage Stir-Fry

Colleen Heatwole, Burton, MI

Makes 6 servings

Prep. Time: 20 minutes ⚬ *Cooking Time: 15 minutes*

¾ lb. 95%-reduced-fat turkey kielbasa, cut into ½-inch-thick slices

½–¾ cup chopped onion

1 cup shredded carrots

8-oz. can unsweetened pineapple chunks, or tidbits

1 Tbsp. arrowroot

½–1 tsp. ground ginger

6 Tbsp. water

⅔ tsp. lower-sodium soy sauce

2 cups hot cooked brown rice

1. In large nonstick skillet, stir-fry sausage 3–4 minutes, or until lightly browned.

2. Add onion and carrots. Stir-fry until crisp-tender.

3. Drain pineapple, reserving juice. Add pineapple to sausage-vegetable mixture.

4. In small bowl, combine arrowroot and ginger. Stir in water, soy sauce, and reserved pineapple juice until smooth.

5. Add sauce to skillet.

6. Bring to boil. Cook, stirring continually 1–2 minutes, or until sauce is thickened.

7. Serve over rice (⅓ cup rice per serving).

Tip:

You can double everything in the recipe except the meat, and it is still excellent.

Calories: 199
Fat: 6 g
Saturated Fat: 2 g
Carbohydrates: 25 g
Fiber: 2 g
Sodium: 592 mg
Protein: 10 g
Cholesterol: 30 mg

Main Dishes: Turkey 🌿 **99**

Quesadilla Casserole

Lorraine Stutzman Amstutz, Akron, PA

Makes 8 servings

Prep. Time: 20 minutes & *Cooking/Baking Time: 35 minutes*

1 lb. ground turkey

½ cup chopped onion

8-oz. can tomato sauce

8-oz. can no-salt-added tomato sauce

15-oz. can black beans, drained

15-oz. can whole-kernel corn, undrained

4½-oz. can chopped green chilies

2 tsp. chili powder

1 tsp. ground cumin

1 tsp. minced garlic

½ tsp. dried oregano

½ tsp. crushed red pepper

8 (8-inch) whole wheat tortillas, *divided*

1 cup 75%-less-fat shredded sharp cheddar cheese, *divided*

1. Brown turkey and onion in skillet. Drain off any drippings.

2. Add tomato sauce, beans, corn, and chilies.

3. Stir in chili powder, cumin, garlic, oregano, and red pepper.

4. Bring to boil; simmer 5 minutes.

5. Spread half of turkey mixture in greased 9 × 13-inch pan.

6. Top with 4 whole wheat tortillas, overlapping as needed.

7. Top with half remaining turkey mixture and half of cheese.

8. Top with remaining tortillas, turkey mixture, and cheese.

9. Bake at 350°F for 15 minutes.

Serving suggestion:

This is great served with chopped lettuce, fresh tomatoes, and avocado, as well as sour cream and salsa as toppings, for each person to add as they wish.

Calories: 338

Fat: 7 g

Saturated Fat: 3 g

Carbohydrates: 39 g

Fiber: 10 g

Sodium: 495 mg

Protein: 32 g

Cholesterol: 37 mg

Turkey Quesadillas

Tara P. Detweiler, Pennsburg, PA

Makes 8 servings

Prep. Time: 10 minutes ⚘ *Cooking/Baking Time: 20 minutes*

1 lb. ground turkey

4 tsp. olive oil

1 large onion, chopped

1 red bell sweet pepper, chopped

4 cloves garlic, chopped

1 tsp. ground cumin

1 tsp. chili powder

1 tsp. dried oregano

15-oz. can tomato sauce, no salt added

15½-oz. can low-sodium kidney, or black, beans, rinsed and drained

8 whole wheat flour tortillas, about 9-inch in diameter

2 Tbsp. parsley

1 tsp. cilantro

½ cup grated cheddar cheese, for topping

1. Cook ground turkey with olive oil and onion in large skillet until turkey is no longer pink.

2. Add red pepper, garlic, and all spices. Cook gently until vegetables are just tender.

3. Stir in tomato sauce and beans. Heat through.

4. Place tortillas on greased cookie sheets. Spoon turkey mixture evenly onto tortillas (approximately ¼ cup per tortilla).

5. Top each with 1 Tbsp. grated cheese.

6. Bake, uncovered, at 400°F for 15 minutes.

Calories: 340

Fat: 10 g

Saturated Fat: 4 g

Carbohydrates: 39 g

Fiber: 10 g

Sodium: 316 mg

Protein: 25 g

Cholesterol: 34 mg

Barbecue Sloppy Joes

STOVETOP

Winifred Paul, Scottdale, PA

Makes 5 sandwiches, 1 per serving

Prep. Time: 10 minutes & Cooking Time: 15 minutes

¾ lb. ground turkey
1 Tbsp. olive oil
1 tsp. lemon juice
1 Tbsp. vinegar
3 Tbsp. water
6 Tbsp. no-sugar-added ketchup
½ tsp. Splenda Brown Sugar Blend
1 tsp. finely chopped onion
⅓ cup chopped celery
1 tsp. dry mustard
5 whole wheat hamburger buns

1. Brown turkey in oil in skillet. Stir frequently to break up clumps and to make sure meat browns completely. Drain off drippings.

2. Make sauce by combining lemon juice, vinegar, water, ketchup, brown sugar, onion, celery, and dry mustard in saucepan.

3. Heat thoroughly, but do not cook enough to soften vegetables.

4. When beginning to simmer, combine with meat. Serve on buns.

Calories: 222
Fat: 6 g
Saturated Fat: 1 g
Carbohydrates: 21 g
Fiber: 2 g
Sodium: 217 mg
Protein: 23 g
Cholesterol: 33 mg

Pork & Beef

Pork Cutlets

STOVETOP

Audrey Romonosky, Austin, TX

Makes 8 servings, 1 cutlet per serving

Prep. Time: 10 minutes & Cooking Time: 20–25 minutes

2 Tbsp. olive oil

½ cup egg substitute

½ cup skim milk

8 pork loin cutlets, about 4 oz. each, fat removed

Salt and pepper

1½ cups panko breadcrumbs

24½-oz. jar lower-sodium marinara sauce

1. Heat oil in large skillet.

2. Beat egg substitute and milk together in shallow dish.

3. Dip cutlets in egg mixture one by one.

4. Place breadcrumbs in another shallow dish.

5. Dredge cutlets in breadcrumbs. Discard leftover liquid and crumb mixtures.

6. Place cutlets in hot oil in skillet, one by one, being careful not to splash yourself.

7. Do not crowd skillet. Cook cutlets in 2 or 3 batches so that they brown and don't just steam in their own juices.

8. Cook each cutlet 3–3½ minutes per side, until browned.

9. Season each side of each cutlet with salt and pepper.

10. Place browned cutlets on a platter. Cover with foil while you cook the next batch.

11. Heat marinara sauce. Spoon over cooked cutlets.

12. Pass any additional sauce to ladle over individual servings.

Serving suggestion:

This would go well with Simple Salted Carrots on page 182, Sweet Potato puree on page 188, Garlic Mushrooms on page 178, or Tasty Beans on page 169.

Tips:

You can make this recipe using chicken cutlets instead.

Calories: 301

Fat: 14 g

Saturated Fat: 4 g

Carbohydrates: 14 g

Fiber: 0.5 g

Sodium: 145 mg

Protein: 28 g

Cholesterol: 79 mg

Ginger Pork Chops

Mary Fisher, Leola, PA

Makes 2 servings

Prep. Time: 10 minutes ☙ *Cooking/Broiling Time: 15 minutes*

2 (6-oz.) bone-in pork loin chops
(4 oz. total meat)
1 tsp. arrowroot
2 Tbsp. low-sodium soy sauce
¼ cup sugar-free honey
1 garlic clove, minced
Dash ground ginger
1 Tbsp. sliced green onion

1. Broil pork chops 3–4 inches from heat for 5–6 minutes on each side.

2. In small saucepan, combine arrowroot and soy sauce until smooth.

3. Stir in sugar-free honey, garlic, and ginger.

4. Bring to a boil. Cook and stir for 1 minute, or until thickened.

5. Drizzle over cooked chops.

6. Sprinkle with green onion just before serving.

Serving suggestion:

This would go well with Sautéed Cabbage on page 186 or Apple Walnut Squash on page 172.

Calories: 488
Fat: 22 g
Saturated Fat: 8 g
Carbohydrates: 37 g
Fiber: 1 g
Sodium: 791 mg
Protein: 38 g
Cholesterol: 100 mg

Sheet Pan Steak & Veggies

Hope Comerford, Clinton Township, MI

Makes 4 servings

Prep. Time: 10 minutes 🍃 *Cooking Time: 8–10 minutes*

1½ lb. 1-inch-thick top sirloin steak

12 oz. broccolini

8 oz. cherry tomatoes, sliced in half

1 yellow bell pepper, sliced into thin strips

2 Tbsp. olive oil

Salt and pepper to taste

¼ tsp. rosemary

¼ tsp. dried thyme

¼ tsp. oregano

1. Preheat the oven to broil.

2. Spray a baking sheet with nonstick spray, then place the steak in the center, with the vegetables around it.

3. Drizzle the olive oil all over everything, making sure to coat all sides of the steak and veggies.

4. Sprinkle with the seasonings, again moving everything around to coat all sides.

5. Place under the broiler. Cook for 4–5 minutes, then flip the steaks over, turn the veggies over, and cook an additional 4–5 minutes.

Calories: 319

Fat: 15 g

Saturated Fat: 4 g

Carbohydrates: 9 g

Fiber: 3 g

Sodium: 132 mg

Protein: 40 g

Cholesterol: 94 mg

INSTANT POT

Quick Steak Tacos

Hope Comerford, Clinton Township, MI

Makes 6 servings

Prep. Time: 5 minutes   Cooking Time: 10 minutes

1 Tbsp. olive oil

8 oz. sirloin steak

2 Tbsp. no-salt steak seasoning

1 tsp. reduced-sodium
Worcestershire sauce

½ red onion, halved and sliced

6 (8-inch) whole wheat tortillas

¼ cup tomatoes

¾ cup reduced-fat Mexican cheese

2 Tbsp. low-fat sour cream

6 Tbsp. garden fresh salsa

¼ cup chopped fresh cilantro

1. Turn the Instant Pot on the Sauté function. When the pot displays "hot," add the olive oil to the pot.

2. Season the steak with the steak seasoning.

3. Add the steak to the pot along with the Worcestershire sauce.

4. Cook each side of the steak for 2–3 minutes until the steak turns brown.

5. Remove the steak from the pot and slice thinly.

6. Add the onion to the pot and cook until translucent with the remaining olive oil and steak juices.

7. Remove the onion from the pot.

8. Warm your tortillas, then assemble your steak, onion, tomatoes, cheese, sour cream, salsa, and cilantro on top of each.

Calories: 262

Fat: 12 g

Saturated Fat: 6 g

Carbohydrates: 22 g

Fiber: 5 g

Sodium: 407 mg

Protein: 16 g

Cholesterol: 36 mg

Meatless

Southwestern Pesto Pasta

Carrie Wood, Paxton, MA

Makes 4–6 servings

Prep. Time: 10 minutes   Cooking Time: 10–12 minutes

1 cup loosely packed cilantro leaves

1 cup loosely packed flat parsley

⅓ cup toasted pepitas (pumpkin seeds)

1 clove garlic, peeled

½ cup crumbled low-fat feta cheese

½ cup extra-virgin olive oil

Salt to taste

1 lb. whole wheat spaghetti or linguine

1. Process all ingredients except pasta in a food processor until a rough paste is formed, adding additional olive oil if the paste seems too dry.

2. Cook spaghetti or linguine according to package directions. Drain.

3. Toss pesto thoroughly with hot pasta and then serve.

Calories: 465
Fat: 28 g
Saturated Fat: 6 g
Carbohydrates: 6 g
Fiber: 6 g
Sodium: 186 mg
Protein: 14 g
Cholesterol: 17 mg

STOVETOP

Zucchini Cakes

Jan McDowell, New Holland, PA
Mary Ann Lefever, Lancaster, PA

Makes 2 main-dish servings

Prep. Time: 15 minutes ⚬ *Cooking Time: 10 minutes*

2 cups zucchini, grated and drained

2 eggs, beaten, or 4 egg whites, or egg substitute equivalent to 2 eggs, or ½ cup soft tofu, blended

¾ cup panko breadcrumbs, *divided*

1 Tbsp. light mayonnaise

¼ tsp. Old Bay seasoning

2 Tbsp. minced onion

Lemon juice, *optional,* not included in analysis

Tartar, or cocktail, sauce, *optional,* not included in analysis

1. In a good-sized bowl, mix zucchini, eggs, egg whites, egg substitute, or tofu, ½ cup breadcrumbs, Old Bay, and onion. Combine thoroughly.

2. Form into golf-ball-sized balls. Flatten and roll lightly in remaining ¼ cup breadcrumbs.

3. Lightly brown on both sides in nonstick pan sprayed with oil.

4. Serve sprinkled with lemon juice, or with tartar or cocktail sauce, if you wish.

Calories: 192

Fat: 8 g

Saturated Fat: 2 g

Carbohydrates: 20 g

Fiber: 2 g

Sodium: 275 mg

Protein: 10 g

Cholesterol: 189 mg

Taco-Ritto

Marlene Fonken, Upland, CA

Makes 4 servings

Prep. Time: 20–25 minutes   *Cooking Time: 5 minutes*

1 Tbsp. + 1 tsp. olive oil

1½ cups broccoli florets

1 cup sliced fresh mushrooms

½ cup chopped green bell pepper

½ cup sliced onion

½ cup diced tomatoes

4 oz. low-fat shredded cheddar, or low-fat pepper jack, cheese

4 (1-oz.) whole wheat flour tortillas, warmed

1. In a skillet, heat oil over medium-high heat. Add broccoli, mushrooms, green peppers, and onion. Stir-fry until tender-crisp, about 2–5 minutes.

2. Remove from heat and stir in tomatoes and cheese. Stir until cheese is partially melted.

3. Divide among the 4 tortillas. Roll up to eat!

Variation:

To add a bit more protein to this dish, use some tofu taco crumbles.

Tip:

Add some taco sauce to Step 2 if you wish.

Calories: 305

Fat: 17 g

Saturated Fat: 8 g

Carbohydrates: 27 g

Fiber: 6 g

Sodium: 410 mg

Protein: 13 g

Cholesterol: 28 mg

STOVETOP

Lemony Quinoa & Chickpeas Bowls

Hope Comerford, Clinton Township, MI

Makes 4–6 servings

Prep. Time: 10 minutes ✣ *Cooking Time: 20 minutes*

¾ cup quinoa

1½ cups water

½ cup lemon juice

¼ cup olive oil

¾ tsp. sea salt

¼ tsp. black pepper

1 tsp. garlic powder

1 tsp. onion powder

15-oz. can chickpeas, rinsed and drained

1 cup cherry tomatoes, sliced in half

¼ cup finely chopped red onion

1 cup chopped English cucumber

1 yellow bell pepper, diced

½ cup pitted kalamata olives, sliced in half

1 cup crumbled low-fat feta

1. In a pot, place the quinoa and water. Bring to a boil, then cover and let simmer for about 15 minutes, or until all the water is absorbed.

2. Meanwhile, make the dressing. In a small bowl, whisk together the lemon juice, olive oil, salt, pepper, onion powder, and garlic powder.

3. When the quinoa is done, divide it among bowls evenly. Evenly divide the chickpeas, cherry tomatoes, onion, cucumber, pepper, kalamata olives, and feta between bowls, on top of the quinoa.

4. Pour the desired amount of lemon dressing on top of each bowl, then serve.

Calories: 347

Fat: 18 g

Saturated Fat: 5 g

Carbohydrates: 35 g

Fiber: 8 g

Sodium: 677 mg

Protein: 13 g

Cholesterol: 22 mg

Seafood

Roasted Salmon

Gloria Julien, Gladstone, MI

Makes 2 servings

Prep. Time: 7–10 minutes ❧ *Baking Time: 10–12 minutes*

2 (5-oz.) pieces salmon with skin
2 tsp. extra-virgin olive oil
1 Tbsp. chopped chives
1 Tbsp. fresh tarragon leaves, *optional*

1. Preheat oven to 425°F.

2. Line a baking sheet with foil.

3. Rub salmon all over with 2 tsp. oil.

4. Roast skin side down on foil-lined baking sheet until fish is cooked through, about 12 minutes. (Check if fish flakes easily with fork after it bakes 10 minutes. Continue baking only if it doesn't.)

5. Using a metal spatula, lift salmon off skin and place salmon on serving plate. Discard skin.

6. Sprinkle salmon with herbs and serve.

Serving suggestion:
This would go well with Rosemary Carrots on page 185 or Roasted Broccoli on page 174.

Calories: 248
Fat: 14 g
Saturated Fat: 2 g
Carbohydrates: 1 g
Fiber: 0 g
Sodium: 64 mg
Protein: 29 g
Cholesterol: 78 mg

OVEN

Nutty Salmon

Mary Seielstad, Sparks, NV

Makes 6 servings

Prep. Time: 5–10 minutes ❧ *Baking Time: 20 minutes*

2 Tbsp. Dijon mustard
2 Tbsp. olive oil
½ cup ground pecans
6 (4-oz.) salmon fillets

1. In a mixing bowl, mix the mustard, oil, and pecans.

2. Spread on salmon fillets.

3. Place on an oiled or baking pan.

4. Bake at 375°F for 15–18 minutes, or until fish flakes easily.

Serving suggestion:
This would go well with Almond Rice on page 190 or Broccoli Dijon on page 175.

Calories: 338
Fat: 26 g
Saturated Fat: 5 g
Carbohydrates: 1 g
Fiber: 1 g
Sodium: 182 mg
Protein: 24 g
Cholesterol: 62 mg

Honey Lemon Garlic Salmon

Judy Gascho, Woodburn, OR

Makes 4 servings

Prep. Time: 15 minutes ✃ *Cooking Time: 8 minutes*

5 Tbsp. olive oil

3 Tbsp. sugar-free honey

2–3 Tbsp. lemon juice

3 cloves garlic, minced

4 (3–4 oz.) fresh salmon fillets

Salt and pepper to taste

1–2 Tbsp. minced parsley
(dried or fresh)

Lemon slices, *optional*

Serving suggestion:
This would go well with Stir-Fried Asparagus on page 179 or Carrots with Dill on page 183.

1. Mix olive oil, honey, lemon juice, and minced garlic in a bowl.

2. Place each piece of salmon on a piece of foil big enough to wrap up the piece of fish.

3. Brush each fillet generously with the olive oil mixture.

4. Sprinkle with salt, pepper, and parsley flakes.

5. Top each with a thin slice of lemon, if desired.

6. Wrap each fillet and seal well at top.

7. Place 1½ cups of water in the inner pot of your Instant Pot and place the trivet in the pot.

8. Place wrapped fillets on the trivet.

9. Close the lid and turn valve to sealing.

10. Cook on Manual at high pressure for 5–8 minutes for smaller pieces, or 10–12 minutes if they are large.

11. Carefully release pressure manually at the end of the cooking time.

12. Unwrap and enjoy.

Calories: 351

Fat: 22 g

Saturated Fat: 4 g

Carbohydrates: 15 g

Fiber: 0 g

Sodium: 81 mg

Protein: 26 g

Cholesterol: 57 mg

OVEN

Flounder Zucchini Bundles

Betty L. Moore, Plano, IL

Makes 4 servings, 1 bundle per serving

Prep. Time: 15 minutes & Baking Time: 20 minutes

4 (6-oz.) flounder fillets
¼ tsp. lemon pepper, *divided*
1 medium lemon, thinly sliced, *divided*
1 medium zucchini, cut into
¼-inch-thick slices, *divided*
12 cherry tomatoes, sliced, *divided*
¼ tsp. dill weed, *divided*
¼ tsp. dried basil, *divided*

1. Place 1 fillet on double thickness of 15 × 18-inch piece of heavy duty foil.

2. Sprinkle with ¼ of lemon pepper.

3. Top with ¼ of lemon slices, zucchini, and tomatoes.

4. Sprinkle with ¼ of dill and basil.

5. Fold foil around fish and seal tightly. Place on baking sheet.

6. Repeat with other fillets.

7. Bake at 425°F for 15–20 minutes, or until fish flakes easily.

Calories: 159
Fat: 3 g
Saturated Fat: 1 g
Carbohydrates: 6 g
Fiber: 2 g
Sodium: 162 mg
Protein: 29 g
Cholesterol: 81 mg

STOVETOP

Easy Tilapia

Karen Ceneviva, New Haven, CT

Makes 4 servings

Prep. Time: 2 minutes ⚬ *Cooking Time: 6–7 minutes*

I Tbsp. olive oil
4 (6-oz.) tilapia fillets
Lemon pepper to taste

1. Heat oil in large skillet.

2. Lay fish in hot skillet, being careful not to splash yourself with hot oil.

3. Sprinkle fish lightly with lemon pepper.

4. Cook 3 minutes.

5. Flip fish carefully. Sprinkle lightly with lemon pepper.

6. Cook another 3 minutes, or just until fish flakes when picked with a fork.

Serving suggestion:

This would go well with Tasty Beans on page 169.

Calories: 193
Fat: 6 g
Saturated Fat: I g
Carbohydrates: 0 g
Fiber: 0 g
Sodium: 109 mg
Protein: 34 g
Cholesterol: 85 mg

Baked Fish

Patricia Howard, Green Valley, AZ

Makes 4 servings

Prep. Time: 5 minutes ⚜ *Baking Time: 10–15 minutes*

4 (4-oz.) fish fillets
(hake, cod, or mahi-mahi)

Juice from ½ lemon

1 tsp. dill weed

1 tsp. dried basil

1 tsp. Mrs. Dash Original
Seasoning Blend

1½ tsp. parsley flakes

4 thin slices lemon

1. Preheat oven to 350°F.

2. Spray baking dish with nonstick cooking spray. Add fish fillets to dish in one layer.

3. Squeeze lemon juice over fish.

4. Sprinkle fish with dill weed, basil, Mrs. Dash seasoning, and parsley.

5. Place lemon slices on top. Cover with foil.

6. Bake 10–15 minutes. Do not overbake. The thinner the fillet, the faster it cooks, and the less time it takes. Check for flakiness with the tines of a fork after 10 minutes. Continue baking only if needed.

Serving suggestion:
This would go well with Zucchini Ribbons on page 171.

Calories: 205
Fat: 12 g
Saturated Fat: 4 g
Carbohydrates: 1 g
Fiber: 0 g
Sodium: 60 mg
Protein: 21 g
Cholesterol: 83 mg

Tuna Tempties

OVEN

Lois Ostrander, Lebanon, PA

Makes 6 servings, 1 sandwich per serving

Prep. Time: 15 minutes ☙ *Baking Time: 15 minutes*

3½ oz. 75%-less-fat cheddar cheese, cubed

6-oz. can low-sodium tuna, flaked

2 Tbsp. chopped green bell pepper

2 Tbsp. minced onion

2 Tbsp. sweet pickle

¼ cup fat-free mayonnaise

Dash pepper

6 whole-grain hot dog buns

1. Combine cheese, tuna, green pepper, minced onion, sweet pickle, mayonnaise, and pepper in mixing bowl.

2. Split buns and fill with tuna mixture.

3. Wrap each bun in foil.

4. Bake in oven at 350°F for 15 minutes until filling is heated and cheese melts.

Calories: 204
Fat: 8 g
Saturated Fat: 3 g
Carbohydrates: 18 g
Fiber: 2 g
Sodium: 440 mg
Protein: 15 g
Cholesterol: 27 mg

Mamma Ree's Faux Cioppino

Maria Shevlin, Sicklerville, NJ

Makes 4 servings

Prep. Time: 10 minutes   Cooking Time: 15 minutes

I Tbsp. olive oil

3–4 cloves garlic, minced

½ cup sliced carrots, cut in half

½ cup sliced celery

½ cup sliced onion

½ cup finely chopped cauliflower

1½ cups low-sodium tomato sauce

½ cup white wine or water

Salt and pepper to taste

3 tsp. parsley flakes

I tsp. garlic powder

I tsp. onion powder

I tsp. Kinder's Red Garlic Seasoning
(if this is unavailable add dried minced
garlic and red pepper flakes)

10–20 large shrimp, shells removed and
sliced in half lengthwise

I cup fat-free half-and-half

1. Set the Instant Pot to Sauté and add the oil. When the oil is heated, add the garlic, carrots, celery, onion, and cauliflower. Sauté until al dente and keep stirring.

2. Add the tomato sauce, wine or water, and seasonings.

3. Simmer for 1–2 minutes over low heat.

4. Place the raw shrimp into the Instant Pot. Stir. Simmer for approximately 3–4 minutes, then add the half-and-half.

Variation:

1. You can add 1/2 cup of green beans and/or diced zucchini in addition to the veggies listed above.

2. You can also add half the amount of shrimp and replace with some small scallops as well.

3. Swap the water for a dry white wine for a more authentic cioppino.

Note:

This recipe can easily be made on the stovetop instead of the Instant Pot.

Calories: 224

Fat: I I g

Saturated Fat: 5 g

Carbohydrates: 6 g

Fiber: 2 g

Sodium: 562 mg

Protein: 16 g

Cholesterol: 128 mg

Shrimp Stir-Fry

Jean Binns Smith, Bellefonte, PA

Makes 4 servings

Prep. Time: 10 minutes   *Cooking Time: 8–10 minutes*

1–2 cloves garlic, chopped

⅛ tsp. grated, or finely chopped, fresh ginger

1 Tbsp. olive oil

2½ cups (about ½ lb.) fresh sugar snap peas

½ cup chopped red bell sweet pepper, *optional*

12 oz. medium-sized raw shrimp, peeled and deveined

1. Sauté garlic and ginger in oil in large skillet until fragrant.

2. Stir in sugar peas and chopped pepper if you wish. Sauté until crisp-tender.

3. Stir in shrimp. Cook over medium heat 3–4 minutes until shrimp are just opaque in centers.

Serving suggestion:

Serve with steamed rice.

Calories: 129

Fat: 4 g

Saturated Fat: 1 g

Carbohydrates: 1 g

Fiber: 0 g

Sodium: 486 mg

Protein: 15 g

Cholesterol: 107 mg

STOVETOP

Shrimp & Zucchini Sauté

Maria Shevlin, Sicklerville, NJ

Makes 3–4 servings

Prep. Time: 10 minutes   Cooking Time: 20 minutes

¼ cup water

1 Tbsp. olive oil

2 carrots, quartered, then sliced into half-inch chunks

3 ribs celery, sliced lengthwise then cut into half-inch chunks

3 cloves garlic, chopped

1 small red onion, chopped

1 small yellow onion, chopped

8 oz. mushrooms, sliced

2 medium zucchini, quartered, then sliced into ½-inch chunks

1 lb. raw medium shrimp, peeled and deveined

Chopped green onions, for garnish

Fresh chopped parsley, for garnish

Sauce:

1 Tbsp. low-sodium soy sauce

½ tsp. black pepper

½ tsp. Morton Salt Substitute

¾ tsp. garlic powder

3-5 Tbsp. reduced-sugar sweet chili sauce

1 Tbsp. sambal oelek (chili paste)

3–7 Tbsp. water

1. Add the water and oil into a large fry pan; toss in the carrots and celery. Cover and steam for about 4 minutes over medium-low heat.

2. Meanwhile, mix the sauce ingredients, then set aside.

3. When you're done steaming the carrots and celery, add in the garlic, onions, and mushrooms; stir. Cook for approximately 5–6 minutes, stirring often.

4. Toss in the zucchini and mix well to combine. Cook 1–2 minutes.

5. Add the sauce along with the shrimp. Mix well. Cover and cook for another 3–5 minutes.

6. Garnish with green onion, fresh parsley, and/or more sambal oelek.

Calories: 222

Fat: 7 g

Saturated Fat: 1 g

Carbohydrates: 17 g

Fiber: 4 g

Sodium: 1239 mg

Protein: 25 g

Cholesterol: 190 mg

STOVETOP

Shrimp Primavera

Elaine Rineer, Lancaster, PA

Makes 4 servings

Prep. Time: 20 minutes   *Cooking Time: 10 minutes*

1 Tbsp. + 1 tsp. olive oil
1½ cups chopped broccoli
½ cup thinly sliced carrots
1 cup sliced mushrooms
2 cloves garlic, minced
1 cup low-sodium chicken broth
1 Tbsp. arrowroot
1 lb. shrimp, peeled and deveined
2 Tbsp. grated low-fat Parmesan cheese
2 Tbsp. parsley

1. In large skillet or wok, sauté broccoli and carrots in oil. Stir-fry until carrots are crisp-tender.

2. Stir in mushrooms and garlic. Stir-fry 1 minute.

3. In a small bowl, whisk together broth and arrowroot. Pour over vegetables.

4. Add shrimp. Cook until shrimp turns pink and sauce thickens.

5. Stir in remaining ingredients.

Calories: 162
Fat: 7 g
Saturated Fat: 1 g
Carbohydrates: 7 g
Fiber: 2 g
Sodium: 736 mg
Protein: 19 g
Cholesterol: 145 mg

Cajun Shrimp

STOVETOP

Mary Ann Potenta, Bridgewater, NJ

Makes 4–5 servings

Prep. Time: 5 minutes ❧ Cooking Time: 10–12 minutes

2–2½ cups uncooked Minute Brown Rice

12 Tbsp. olive oil buttery spread, *divided*

½ cup chopped green onions

1 tsp. minced garlic

1 tsp. cayenne pepper

½ tsp. white pepper

½ tsp. black pepper

¼ tsp. dry mustard

½ tsp. salt

1 tsp. Tabasco sauce

2 lb. shrimp, peeled and cleaned

1. Begin by preparing the Minute Brown Rice according to the box directions. Once it is cooking, proceed with the following steps.

2. Melt 8 Tbsp. of olive oil buttery spread in large skillet. Add onions and garlic and sauté till clear, but not brown, about 1 minute.

3. Add peppers, mustard, and salt. Cook and stir for 3 minutes.

4. Mix in 4 Tbsp. of olive oil buttery spread and Tabasco sauce until blended.

5. Add shrimp. Cook just until pink. Do not overcook.

6. Serve over cooked rice.

Note:

This is hot! You can tone things down by reducing the amounts of the peppers and the Tabasco sauce.

Calories: 448

Fat: 25 g

Saturated Fat: 7 g

Carbohydrates: 28 g

Fiber: 2 g

Sodium: 1333 mg

Protein: 28 g

Cholesterol: 229 mg

Salads

BLT Salad

Alica Denlinger, Lancaster, PA

Makes 12 servings, about 3½ oz. per serving

Prep. Time: 30 minutes

2 heads Romaine lettuce, torn

2 cups sliced cherry tomatoes

4 bacon strips, cooked and crumbled

½ cup freshly grated low-fat
Parmesan cheese

Dressing:

¼ cup olive oil

½ tsp. Morton Salt Substitute

½ tsp. pepper

¼ cup fresh lemon juice

2 cloves garlic, crushed

1. Toss together salad ingredients in a large bowl.

2. Shake together dressing ingredients.

3. Pour dressing over salad immediately before serving.

Calories: 68

Fat: 6 g

Saturated Fat: 1 g

Carbohydrates: 3 g

Fiber: 1 g

Sodium: 80 mg

Protein: 2 g

Cholesterol: 4 mg

Festive Apple Salad

Susan Kasting, Jenks, OK

Makes 8 servings, about 5 oz. per serving

Prep. Time: 15 minutes

Dressing:

2 Tbsp. olive oil

2 Tbsp. vinegar or lemon juice

2 Tbsp. Dijon mustard

1½–3 Tbsp. Splenda Zero Calorie Granulated Sweetener

Salt and pepper to taste

4–6 Tbsp. chopped walnuts or cashews

1 Granny Smith apple, chopped

1 large head Romaine lettuce, chopped

4 Tbsp. crumbled low-fat blue cheese, or shredded baby Swiss, *optional*

1. In the bottom of a large salad bowl, make dressing by mixing the oil, vinegar or lemon juice, mustard, Splenda, salt, and pepper.

2. Add the apple and nuts and stir to coat. Put lettuce and blue cheese on top without stirring.

3. Mix it all together when ready to serve.

Tip:

You can serve the dressing on the side.

—Mary Ann Bowman, Ephrata, PA

Calories: 114

Fat: 8 g

Saturated Fat: 1 g

Carbohydrates: 9 g

Fiber: 1 g

Sodium: 87 mg

Protein: 1 g

Cholesterol: 0 mg

Orange-Spinach Salad

Esther Shisler, Lansdale, PA

Makes 8 servings, about 7 oz. per serving

Prep. Time: 25 minutes

Honey-Caraway Dressing:

¾ cup low-fat mayonnaise

2 Tbsp. sugar-free honey

1 Tbsp. lemon juice

1 Tbsp. caraway seeds

10-oz. bag spinach or Romaine lettuce

1 medium head iceberg lettuce, shredded

2 Tbsp. diced onion

2 Tbsp. diced canned pimento or red pepper

2 large oranges, peeled and chopped

1 small cucumber, sliced

1. In small bowl, whisk mayonnaise, honey, lemon juice, and caraway seeds until blended. Cover and refrigerate. Stir before using.

2. Into large salad bowl, tear spinach into bite-sized pieces.

3. Add lettuce, onion, pimento, oranges, and cucumber. Toss gently with dressing.

Serving suggestion:
Pasta dishes go well with this salad.

Calories: 103
Fat: 5 g
Saturated Fat: 1 g
Carbohydrates: 14 g
Fiber: 2 g
Sodium: 191 mg
Protein: 1 g
Cholesterol: 4 mg

Spinach Salad

Ruth Zercher, Grantham, PA

Makes 15 servings

Prep. Time: 20 minutes

I lb. fresh spinach with stems discarded

I head Bibb lettuce

¼ cup unsalted cashew nuts, *divided*

½ cup olive oil

I tsp. celery seed

2 Tbsp. Splenda Zero Calorie
Granulated Sweetener

I tsp. Morton Salt Substitute

I tsp. dry mustard

I tsp. grated onion

3 Tbsp. vinegar

1. Wash spinach and lettuce and tear into bite-sized pieces. Combine spinach, lettuce, and nuts in serving bowl, reserving a few nuts for garnish.

2. Combine all other ingredients in blender and mix well.

3. Immediately before serving, pour dressing over greens and nuts. Sprinkle reserved nuts over top.

Calories: 92

Fat: 8 g

Saturated Fat: I g

Carbohydrates: 3 g

Fiber: I g

Sodium: 25 mg

Protein: I g

Cholesterol: 0 mg

STOVETOP

Lettuce Salad with Hot Bacon Dressing

Mary B. Sensenig, New Holland, PA

Makes 12 servings, about 3 oz. lettuce and 2 Tbsp. dressing per serving

Prep. Time: 5 minutes   ✿   Cooking Time: 15 minutes

5 pieces bacon

¼ cup Splenda Zero Calorie Granulated Sweetener

1 Tbsp. arrowroot

½ tsp. Morton Salt Substitute

1 beaten egg

1 cup fat-free milk

¼ cup vinegar

36 oz. ready-to-serve mixed lettuces, or 2 medium heads iceberg lettuce

1. Sauté bacon in skillet until crisp.

2. Remove bacon from heat and drain. Chop. Discard drippings.

3. Add Splenda, arrowroot, and salt substitute to skillet. Blend well.

4. Add egg, milk, and vinegar, stirring until smooth.

5. Cook over low heat, stirring continually until thickened and smooth.

6. When dressing is no longer hot, but still warm, toss with torn lettuce leaves and chopped bacon.

7. Serve immediately.

Calories: 111

Fat: 7 g

Saturated Fat: 2 g

Carbohydrates: 8 g

Fiber: 1 g

Sodium: 127 mg

Protein: 4 g

Cholesterol: 26 mg

Grilled Fiesta Chicken Salad

Liz Clapper, Lancaster, PA

Makes 4 main-dish servings

Prep. Time: 10 minutes 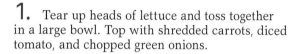 Cooking Time: 20 minutes

I head Bibb lettuce
I head red leaf lettuce
I cup shredded carrots
I medium tomato, diced
2 green onions, chopped
I lb. boneless, skinless chicken breasts
I tsp. chili powder
I sweet red bell pepper
I Tbsp. olive oil
I cup thawed frozen corn
½ cup shredded low-fat cheddar cheese
8 Tbsp. fat-free ranch dressing
2 whole wheat pita breads, 4-inch diameter

Tip

You can bake pitas at 375°F in oven for 10 minutes instead of grilling.

1. Tear up heads of lettuce and toss together in a large bowl. Top with shredded carrots, diced tomato, and chopped green onions.

2. Season chicken with chili powder. Grill chicken 3–4 minutes on each side.

3. Meanwhile, dice red pepper. Toss with olive oil and cook in a medium skillet over medium heat for 2 minutes.

4. Add corn and cook for 1 more minute.

5. When chicken has cooled to room temperature, dice chicken.

6. Top salad with diced chicken.

7. Spoon corn and pepper over top.

8. Sprinkle with cheese. Drizzle each salad with 2 Tbsp. dressing.

9. Grill whole wheat pitas for 2–3 minutes each side. Cut into fourths. Serve 2 wedges with each individual salad.

Calories: 434
Fat: 15 g
Saturated Fat: 6 g
Carbohydrates: 39 g
Fiber: 5 g
Sodium: 677 mg
Protein: 38 g
Cholesterol: 105 mg

Two-Cheese Tossed Salad

Elaine Hoover, Leola, PA

Makes 8 servings, about 5 oz. per serving

Prep. Time: 20 minutes

10 cups spinach and Romaine lettuce, chopped

½ lb. mushrooms, sliced

8 oz. fat-free cottage cheese

10 strips bacon, fried and crumbled

Dressing:

¼ cup olive oil

½ cup minced red onion

2 Tbsp. Splenda Zero Calorie Granulated Sweetener

¼ cup vinegar

1 tsp. poppy seed

½ tsp. prepared mustard

¼ tsp. salt

2 oz. reduced-fat shredded Swiss cheese

1. Layer in a large serving bowl: half of the spinach/lettuce, half mushrooms, half cottage cheese, and half bacon. Repeat layers.

2. Combine dressing ingredients together in a shaker or lidded jar and shake well.

3. Add dressing and Swiss cheese just before serving.

Calories: 313

Fat: 26 g

Saturated Fat: 7 g

Carbohydrates: 9 g

Fiber: 1 g

Sodium: 500 mg

Protein: 11 g

Cholesterol: 34 mg

NO-COOK

Italian Green Salad

Jane Geigley, Lancaster, PA

Makes 4 servings, about 7 oz. per serving

Prep. Time: 10 minutes

16-oz. pkg. green salad mix

1 oz. pastrami, chopped in ½-inch pieces

¼ cup shredded part-skim mozzarella cheese

4 plum tomatoes, chopped

1 tsp. Italian herb seasoning

3 Tbsp. fat-free Italian salad dressing

¼ cup sliced ripe olives

1. Combine salad mix, pastrami, mozzarella, tomatoes, and seasoning.

2. Drizzle with salad dressing; toss to coat.

3. Before serving, top with olives. Serve immediately.

Calories: 75

Fat: 3 g

Saturated Fat: 1 g

Carbohydrates: 39 g

Fiber: 3 g

Sodium: 442 mg

Protein: 38 g

Cholesterol: 10 mg

Confetti Salad

Beth Guntlisbergen, Green Bay, WI

Makes 6 servings

Prep. Time: 20 minutes

2 cups shredded red cabbage

15½-oz. can white (cannellini) beans, rinsed and drained

11-oz. can mandarin oranges, drained

⅓ cup walnuts, toasted

2 large green onions with green tops, sliced

3 Tbsp. olive oil

2 Tbsp. balsamic vinegar

2 Tbsp. freshly squeezed orange juice (approx. ½ orange)

Pepper to taste

1. Put first 5 ingredients in a bowl.

2. Place olive oil, vinegar, juice, and pepper in a jar with a tight-fitting lid. Shake until thoroughly mixed.

3. Toss everything together.

4. Serve immediately.

Calories: 241
Fat: 12 g
Saturated Fat: 1 g
Carbohydrates: 28 g
Fiber: 6 g
Sodium: 14 mg
Protein: 9 g
Cholesterol: 0 mg

Greek Pasta Salad

Edie Moran, West Babylon, NY
Judi Manos, West Islip, NY

Makes 8 servings, about 4½ oz. per serving

Prep. Time: 15 minutes ⚘ *Cooking Time for Pasta: 15 minutes*

2 cups cooked whole wheat pasta,
  rinsed and cooled (1 cup dry)

4 medium plum tomatoes, chopped

15-oz. can garbanzo beans,
  rinsed and drained

1 medium onion, chopped

6-oz. can pitted black olives, drained

1 oz. crumbled reduced-fat feta cheese

1 clove garlic, minced

¼ cup olive oil

2 Tbsp. lemon juice

½ tsp. salt

½ tsp. pepper

1. In a large bowl, combine macaroni, tomatoes, garbanzo beans, onion, olives, and feta cheese.

2. In a small bowl, whisk together garlic, oil, lemon juice, salt, and pepper. Pour over salad and toss to coat.

3. Cover and chill in refrigerator. Stir before serving.

Calories: 200

Fat: 11 g

Saturated Fat: 2 g

Carbohydrates: 21 g

Fiber: 5 g

Sodium: 391 mg

Protein: 6 g

Cholesterol: 3 mg

Chicken Pasta Salad

Esther Gingerich, Kalona, IA

Makes 10 servings, about 7 oz. per serving

Prep. Time: 15 minutes   Chill Time: 1 hour

2¼ cups diced cooked chicken

2 cups cooked small whole wheat pasta or macaroni (1 cup dry)

2 cups diced celery

2 cups seedless grape halves

4 hard-boiled eggs, diced

15-oz. can unsweetened pineapple tidbits, drained

Dressing:

¾ cup low-fat mayonnaise

½ cup fat-free sour cream

½ cup fat-free frozen whipped topping, thawed

1 Tbsp. lemon juice

1 Tbsp. Splenda Zero Calorie Granulated Sweetener

½ tsp. salt

½ cup cashew pieces

1. In a large bowl, combine chicken, macaroni, celery, grapes, eggs, and pineapple.

2. Whisk dressing ingredients until smooth. Pour dressing over salad; toss to coat.

3. Chill at least one hour. Just before serving, fold in cashews.

Tip:

It's simple to put this together if chicken is cooked and diced, macaroni is cooked, and eggs are boiled ahead of time.

Calories: 240

Fat: 6 g

Saturated Fat: 2 g

Carbohydrates: 30 g

Fiber: 3 g

Sodium: 319 mg

Protein: 16 g

Cholesterol: 103 mg

Summer Salad

June S. Groff, Denver, PA

Makes 8 servings, about 6 oz. per serving

Prep. Time: 20 minutes   ⚬   Cooking Time for Couscous: 10 minutes

1½ cups cooked garbanzo beans

½ cup chopped onion

½ cup chopped celery

½ cup chopped cucumber

½ cup chopped red grapes

2 medium tomatoes, chopped

2.2-oz. can sliced black olives, drained

¾ cup couscous, cooked and cooled

Dressing:

½ cup olive oil

½ cup lemon juice or vinegar

⅛ tsp. minced garlic

1 Tbsp. Dijon mustard

¼ tsp. dried oregano

¼ tsp. dried basil

1 Tbsp. Splenda Zero Calorie Granulated Sweetener

⅛ tsp. coriander

⅛ tsp. onion powder

1 tsp. dried parsley

2 Tbsp. freshly grated low-fat Parmesan cheese

1. Toss salad ingredients together.

2. Mix the dressing ingredients together. Pour dressing over salad mixture and toss.

3. Top with Parmesan cheese.

Calories: 230

Fat: 16 g

Saturated Fat: 2 g

Carbohydrates: 19 g

Fiber: 4 g

Sodium: 133 mg

Protein: 4 g

Cholesterol: 1 mg

Curried Chicken Salad

Bonita Stutzman, Harrisonburg, VA

Makes 10 main-dish servings

Prep. Time: 20 minutes

1 cup fat-free mayonnaise

¾ cup plain nonfat yogurt

2 Tbsp. sugar-free honey

1 Tbsp. lemon juice

1½ Tbsp. curry powder

6 cups chopped cooked chicken, cooled

3 cups halved red grapes

¾ cup toasted slivered almonds

¾ cup diced celery

Romaine or Bibb lettuce

1. Mix together first five ingredients in a medium bowl.

2. In a large bowl, toss together chicken, grapes, almonds, and celery.

3. Pour dressing over chicken mixture and toss.

4. Refrigerate until serving time.

5. Serve on a bed of Romaine lettuce.

Calories: 262

Fat: 7 g

Saturated Fat: 1 g

Carbohydrates: 19 g

Fiber: 3 g

Sodium: 269 mg

Protein: 30 g

Cholesterol: 72 mg

STOVETOP

Asparagus, Apple & Chicken Salad

Betty Salch, Bloomington, IL
Wilma Stoltzfus, Honey Brook, PA

Makes 3–4 servings

Prep. Time: 20 minutes & Cooking Time: 3–4 minutes

1 cup fresh asparagus, cut
into 1-inch-long pieces

2 Tbsp. cider vinegar

2 Tbsp. vegetable oil

2 tsp. sugar-free honey

2 tsp. minced fresh parsley

½ tsp. salt

¼ tsp. pepper

1 cup cubed cooked chicken

½ cup diced red apples, unpeeled

2 cups torn mixed greens

Alfalfa sprouts, *optional*

1. In a small saucepan, cook asparagus in a small amount of water until crisp-tender, about 3–4 minutes. Drain and cool.

2. In a good-sized mixing bowl, combine the next 6 ingredients.

3. Stir in the chicken, apples, and asparagus. Toss.

4. Serve over greens. Garnish with alfalfa sprouts if you wish.

Calories: 161

Fat: 8 g

Saturated Fat: 1 g

Carbohydrates: 11 g

Fiber: 2 g

Sodium: 268 mg

Protein: 12 g

Cholesterol: 30 mg

Edamame Salad

Esther Porter, Minneapolis, MN

Makes 4 servings

Prep. Time: 15–20 minutes

¼ cup seasoned rice vinegar

1 Tbsp. olive oil

⅛ tsp. black pepper

16 oz. fresh, or frozen, soybeans (thawed if frozen)

Garnish:

Sliced radishes

Fresh cilantro leaves

1. Mix the rice vinegar, oil, and black pepper. Pour over soybeans in a large bowl.

2. Garnish with radishes and cilantro.

3. Chill and serve.

Serving suggestion:
This is good over low-fat cottage cheese.

Calories: 186

Fat: 9 g

Saturated Fat: 1 g

Carbohydrates: 14 g

Fiber: 6 g

Sodium: 249 mg

Protein: 14 g

Cholesterol: 0 mg

My Brother's Black Bean Salad

Shirley Hedman, Schenectady, NY

Makes 16 servings

Prep. Time: 20 minutes

2 (15-oz.) cans low-sodium black beans

¾ cup corn, fresh, frozen, or canned

1 cup chopped red sweet bell pepper

¾ cup chopped red onion

4–6 cloves minced garlic, according to your taste preference

½ cup chopped fresh cilantro

1 minced jalapeño, or 4-oz. can chopped green chilies

⅓ cup olive oil

½ cup lemon juice

¼ tsp. white pepper

1. Rinse and drain the beans, and the corn if it's canned. (If you're using fresh or frozen corn, you don't need to cook it.)

2. Mix all ingredients in a large bowl.

3. Serve immediately, or refrigerate until 2 hours before serving. Remove from fridge and serve at room temperature.

Calories: 80

Fat: 5 g

Saturated Fat: 1 g

Carbohydrates: 8 g

Fiber: 2 g

Sodium: 38 mg

Protein: 2 g

Cholesterol: 0 mg

Sour Cream Cucumber Salad

Mary Jones, Marengo, OH

Makes 6 servings, about 5 oz. per serving

Prep. Time: 20–30 minutes

3 medium cucumbers, about 9 oz. each, unpeeled and sliced thinly

½ tsp. salt

½ cup finely chopped green onions

1 Tbsp. white vinegar

Dash pepper, *optional*

¼ cup fat-free sour cream

1. Sprinkle cucumber with salt. Let stand 15 minutes. Drain liquid.

2. Add onions, vinegar, and pepper.

3. Just before serving, stir in sour cream.

Calories: 34

Fat: 0 g

Saturated Fat: 0 g

Carbohydrates: 8 g

Fiber: 1 g

Sodium: 179 mg

Protein: 1 g

Cholesterol: 1 mg

White Rabbit Salad

Esther Nafziger, Bluffton, OH

Makes 6 main-dish servings

Prep. Time: 20 minutes

2 small apples, unpeeled and chopped

½ cup raisins

½ cup walnuts, chopped and toasted

¼ cup sunflower seeds, toasted

2 Tbsp. poppy seeds

1½ cups low-fat (1%) cottage cheese

2 Tbsp. sugar-free honey

Juice of ½ lemon

Lettuce leaves

1. Mix apples, raisins, walnuts, and sunflower and poppy seeds together in a mixing bowl.

2. In a separate bowl, mix the cottage cheese, honey, and lemon juice.

3. Gently mix fruit and nut mixture with cottage cheese mixture.

4. Serve very cold on lettuce greens.

Variation:

Optional fruits, to be cut and added, or substituted, for apples:
- *fresh firm pears*
- *peaches*
- *green grapes*
- *orange sections*

Calories: 246
Fat: 11 g
Saturated Fat: 1 g
Carbohydrates: 29 g
Fiber: 4 g
Sodium: 234 mg
Protein: 11 g
Cholesterol: 2 mg

Grape Broccoli Salad

Robin Schrock, Millersburg, OH

Makes 15 servings

Prep. Time: 30 minutes

6 cups fresh broccoli florets

6 green onions, sliced

I cup diced celery

2 cups halved green grapes

I cup low-fat mayonnaise

⅓ cup Splenda Zero Calorie Granulated Sweetener

I Tbsp. cider vinegar

I cup slivered almonds, toasted

1. In a large salad bowl, combine broccoli, onions, celery, and grapes.

2. In another bowl, whisk together mayonnaise, Splenda, and vinegar.

3. Pour dressing over broccoli mixture and toss to coat.

4. Cover and refrigerate until serving. Stir in almonds just before serving.

Calories: 87

Fat: 5 g

Saturated Fat: 0 g

Carbohydrates: 10 g

Fiber: 2 g

Sodium: 157 mg

Protein: 3 g

Cholesterol: 0 mg

Vegetables & Side Dishes

Tasty Beans

Linda Yoder, Fresno, OH

Makes 6 servings, about 4½ oz. per serving

Prep. Time: 5 minutes   Cooking Time: 10 minutes

I cup thinly sliced onion

I clove garlic, minced

4 oz. fresh or canned mushrooms, sliced

I Tbsp. olive oil

2 pints (4 cups) frozen green beans, partially thawed

½ tsp. salt

I Tbsp. dill seeds

Dash cayenne pepper

¾ cup water

1. Sauté onion and garlic, plus fresh mushrooms if using, in olive oil just until tender but not brown.

2. Add green beans, salt, dill seeds, cayenne pepper, and water and bring to boil.

3. Reduce heat; cover. Simmer until beans are crisp-tender.

Tips:

1. May be doubled. Best if it can be cooked just before the meal.

2. Garnish with sliced almonds for more color and crunch.

Serving suggestion:

This would go well with Pork Cutlets on page 107 or Easy Tilapia on page 128.

Calories: 67

Fat: 3 g

Saturated Fat: 0 g

Carbohydrates: I0 g

Fiber: 4 g

Sodium: I63 mg

Protein: 3 g

Cholesterol: 0 mg

Tangy Green Beans

Mary B. Sensenig, New Holland, PA

Makes 10 servings

Prep. Time: 5 minutes   *Cooking Time: 8–10 minutes*

1 ½ lb. green beans, fresh,
frozen, or canned

⅓ cup diced sweet red bell peppers

4½ tsp. olive oil

4½ tsp. water

1 ½ tsp. vinegar

1 ½ tsp. prepared mustard

¼ tsp. salt

¼ tsp. pepper

⅛ tsp. garlic powder

1. Cook beans and red peppers in a steamer basket over water until crisp-tender.

2. Whisk together all remaining ingredients in a small bowl.

3. Transfer beans to a serving bowl. Add dressing and stir to coat.

Serving suggestion:

This would go well with Basil Chicken Strips on page 84.

Calories: 44

Fat: 2 g

Saturated Fat: 0 g

Carbohydrates: 6 g

Fiber: 2 g

Sodium: 57 mg

Protein: 1 g

Cholesterol: 0 mg

Zucchini Ribbons

Delores Gnagey, Saginaw, MI

Makes 4 servings

Prep. Time: 15 minutes   Cooking Time: 9 minutes

1 large zucchini, unpeeled, ends trimmed

1 Tbsp. olive oil

3 cloves garlic, minced

1 cup cherry tomato halves

½ tsp. dried basil

Pepper to taste

1. With vegetable peeler, slice zucchini into long, lengthwise strips, thick enough not to bend. (If strips are too thin, they'll get mushy while sautéing.)

2. Heat oil in large skillet over medium heat. Add zucchini ribbons. Sauté 4 minutes.

3. Add garlic and sauté 2 more minutes.

4. Add cherry tomatoes and sauté 2 additional minutes.

5. Sprinkle with basil and pepper to taste. Cook 1 minute.

Serving suggestion:

This would go well with Lemon Grilled Chicken Breasts on page 73 or Baked Fish on page 129.

Calories: 44

Fat: 4 g

Saturated Fat: 0.5 g

Carbohydrates: 3 g

Fiber: 1 g

Sodium: 4 mg

Protein: 1 g

Cholesterol: 0 mg

Apple Walnut Squash

Michele Ruvola, Selden, NY

Makes 4 servings

Prep. Time: 10 minutes   Cooking Time: 5 minutes

I cup water

2 small (1¼ pound each) acorn squash

2 Tbsp. brown sugar

Brown sugar substitute to equal I Tbsp. sugar

2 Tbsp. light, soft tub margarine

3 Tbsp. light apple juice

1½ tsp. ground cinnamon

¼ tsp. salt

I cup toasted walnuts halves

I medium apple, unpeeled, chopped

1. Pour water into Instant Pot and place the trivet inside.

2. Cut squash crosswise in half. Remove seeds. Place in the Instant Pot on top of the trivet, cut sides up.

3. Combine brown sugar, brown sugar substitute, margarine, apple juice, cinnamon, and salt. Spoon into squash.

4. Secure the lid and make sure vent is set to sealing. Press Manual and set time for 5 minutes.

5. Let the pressure release naturally.

6. Combine walnuts and chopped apple. Add to center of squash before serving.

Serving suggestion:
This would go well with Ginger Pork Chops on page 108.

Calories: 403

Fat: 25 g

Saturated Fat: 3 g

Carbohydrates: 46 g

Fiber: 8 g

Sodium: 558 mg

Protein: 7 g

Cholesterol: 0 mg

OVEN

Roasted Broccoli

Andrea Cunningham, Arlington, KS

Makes 4 servings

Prep. Time: 10 minutes ✂ *Baking Time: 20 minutes*

1 head (about 5 cups) broccoli, cut into long pieces all the way through (you will eat the stems)

1 Tbsp. olive oil

2–3 cloves garlic, sliced thin

Pepper to taste

Lemon wedges

1. Preheat oven to 400°F.

2. Place broccoli in baking pan with sides. Drizzle with olive oil. Toss to coat.

3. Sprinkle garlic and pepper over top.

4. Transfer to oven and roast 15–20 minutes, or until broccoli is crispy on the ends and a little browned.

5. Sprinkle with lemon juice.

Serving suggestion:

This would go well with Buttery Lemon Chicken on page 74 or Roasted Salmon on page 123.

Calories: 38

Fat: 3 g

Saturated Fat: 0 g

Carbohydrates: 8 g

Fiber: 1 g

Sodium: 8 mg

Protein: 1 g

Cholesterol: 0 mg

Broccoli Dijon

Jean Butzer, Batavia, NY

Makes 4 servings

Prep. Time: 15 minutes ❧ Cooking Time: 10 minutes

1½ lb. broccoli
2 Tbsp. olive oil
1 medium onion, finely chopped
2 cloves garlic, finely chopped
½ cup fat-free sour cream
1 Tbsp. Dijon mustard
1 Tbsp. lemon juice
Pepper to taste

1. Cut broccoli into florets. Peel and slice the stalks. Steam or boil in water in saucepan until tender, but still firm and bright green. Drain, and keep warm.

2. Meanwhile heat oil in a skillet over moderate heat. Sauté onion and garlic until tender but not brown, about 5 minutes.

3. Add remaining ingredients to skillet and stir over low heat.

4. Place broccoli in serving dish. Spoon sauce over top. Serve immediately.

Serving suggestion:
This would go well with Turkey Steaks Dijon on page 98 or Nutty Salmon on page 124.

Calories: 152
Fat: 7 g
Saturated Fat: 1 g
Carbohydrates: 19 g
Fiber: 5 g
Sodium: 189 mg
Protein: 6 g
Cholesterol: 3 mg

Italian-Style Broccoli

Shirley Hedman, Schenectady, NY

Makes 4–6 servings

Prep. Time: 10 minutes & Cooking Time: 10 minutes

4 cups broccoli florets
I Tbsp. olive oil
2 cloves garlic, minced or crushed
¼ tsp. red pepper flakes
I tsp. grated low-fat Parmesan cheese

1. Steam broccoli for 3 minutes in nonstick pan. Remove from pan and wipe pan dry.

2. Add olive oil, garlic, and red pepper flakes to pan. Cook slowly, about 3 minutes.

3. Add broccoli and shake in pan to cook evenly.

4. Sprinkle with grated cheese and serve warm.

Serving suggestion:
This would go well with Lemon Grilled Chicken Breasts on page 73.

Calories: 43
Fat: 3 g
Saturated Fat: 0 g
Carbohydrates: 4 g
Fiber: 2 g
Sodium: 25 mg
Protein: 2 g
Cholesterol: 0 mg

Garlic Mushrooms

Lizzie Ann Yoder, Hartville, OH

Makes 4 servings, about ½ cup per serving

Prep. Time: 20 minutes ⚗ *Cooking Time: 15–20 minutes*

3 Tbsp. olive oil buttery spread
2 cloves garlic, minced
1 lb. mushrooms, sliced
4 green onions, chopped
1 tsp. lemon juice

1. In a skillet, melt the buttery spread and sauté the garlic briefly.

2. Add mushrooms, scallions, and lemon juice and cook, stirring, about 10 minutes.

Serving suggestion:
This would go well with French Onion Chicken on page 75 or Pork Cutlets on page 107.

Calories: 99
Fat: 7 g
Saturated Fat: 2 g
Carbohydrates: 8 g
Fiber: 3 g
Sodium: 61 mg
Protein: 3 g
Cholesterol: 0 mg

Stir-Fried Asparagus

STOVETOP

Sylvia Beiler, Lowville, NY

Makes 6 servings

Prep. Time: 5 minutes ❧ *Cooking Time: 2–3 minutes*

I Tbsp. olive oil
3 cups asparagus, sliced diagonally
4 green onions, sliced diagonally
I clove garlic, minced, *optional*
I tsp. lemon juice

1. Heat oil in pan. Add sliced vegetables and garlic.

2. Stir-fry until crisp-tender.

3. Sprinkle with lemon juice. Serve immediately.

Serving suggestion:
This would go well with Honey Lemon Garlic Salmon on page 125 or Buttery Lemon Chicken on page 74.

Calories: 37
Fat: 2 g
Saturated Fat: 0 g
Carbohydrates: 4 g
Fiber: 2 g
Sodium: 3 mg
Protein: 2 g
Cholesterol: 0 mg

Roasted Asparagus

Barbara Walker, Sturgis, SD

Makes 6 servings

Prep. Time: 5 minutes ❧ *Cooking Time: 12 minutes*

1 lb. fresh asparagus spears
2–3 Tbsp. olive oil
⅛ tsp. pepper
2 Tbsp. balsamic vinegar

1. Place asparagus in bowl with olive oil. Toss together to coat asparagus.

2. Place asparagus spears on a baking sheet in a single layer. Sprinkle with pepper.

3. Roast uncovered at 450°F. Shake pan once or twice to turn spears after about 6 minutes.

4. Roast another 6 minutes, or until asparagus is tender-crisp.

5. Put on a plate and drizzle with balsamic vinegar. Serve immediately.

Tip:

The asparagus spears may need more or less roasting time, depending on their size and thickness.

Serving suggestion:

This would go well with Encore Dijon Chicken on page 78.

Calories: 59
Fat: 5 g
Saturated Fat: 1 g
Carbohydrates: 4 g
Fiber: 2 g
Sodium: 3 mg
Protein: 2 g
Cholesterol: 0 mg

Simple Salted Carrots

Hope Comerford, Clinton Township, MI

Makes 4 servings

Prep. Time: 5 minutes   Cooking Time: 2 minutes

1 lb. package baby carrots
1 cup water
1 tsp. olive oil buttery spread
Sea salt to taste

1. Combine the carrots and water in the inner pot of the Instant Pot.

2. Seal the lid and make sure the vent is on sealing. Select manual for 2 minutes.

3. When cooking time is done, release the pressure manually then pour the carrots into a strainer.

4. Wipe the inner pot dry. Select the sauté function and add the buttery spread.

5. When the buttery spread is melted, add the carrots back into the inner pot and sauté them until they are coated well with the buttery spread.

6. Remove the carrots and sprinkle them with the sea salt to taste before serving.

Serving suggestion:

This would go well with Pork Cutlets on page 107 or Turkey Steaks Dijon on page 98.

Calories: 72
Fat: 3 g
Saturated Fat: 05 g
Carbohydrates: 11 g
Fiber: 3 g
Sodium: 113 mg
Protein: 1 g
Cholesterol: 0 mg

Carrots with Dill

Marilyn Mowry, Irving, TX

Makes 4 servings

Prep. Time: 5 minutes ✃ *Cooking Time: 12–15 minutes*

4 cups water

2 cups peeled and sliced fresh carrots

1 Tbsp. soft tub margarine, non-hydrogenated

2 Tbsp. sugar-free honey

¼ tsp. Lawry's Lemon Pepper

¼ tsp. salt, *optional*

⅛–¼ tsp. dill weed

1. Bring 4 cups water to a boil in saucepan. Add carrots. Cover and boil 1 minute.

2. Drain carrots. Add remaining ingredients to carrots in saucepan and mix well. Heat through over low heat.

3. Stir again and spoon into serving dish.

Serving suggestion:

This would go well with Honey Lemon Garlic Salmon on page 125.

Calories: 82
Fat: 3 g
Saturated Fat: 0.5 g
Carbohydrates: 15 g
Fiber: 2 g
Sodium: 96 mg
Protein: 1 g
Cholesterol: 0 mg

Rosemary Carrots

Orpha Herr, Andover, NY

Makes 6 servings

Prep. Time: 15 minutes ☙ *Cooking Time: 15–20 minutes*

1½ lb. carrots, sliced

1 Tbsp. olive oil

½ cup diced green sweet bell peppers

1 tsp. dried rosemary, crushed

¼ tsp. coarsely ground pepper

1. In a skillet cook and stir carrots in oil 10–12 minutes, or until tender-crisp.

2. Add green pepper. Cook and stir 5 minutes, or until carrots and green peppers are tender, but not too soft.

3. Sprinkle with rosemary and pepper. Heat through.

Serving suggestion:

This would go well with Baked Fish on page 129 or Roasted Salmon on page 123.

Calories: 70

Fat: 3 g

Saturated Fat: 0 g

Carbohydrates: 12 g

Fiber: 3 g

Sodium: 79 mg

Protein: 1 g

Cholesterol: 0 mg

STOVETOP

Sautéed Cabbage

Laverne Nafziger, Goshen, IN

Makes 6 servings

Prep. Time: 15 minutes ⚭ *Cooking Time: 15–20 minutes*

1 Tbsp. olive oil
1 Tbsp. mustard seed
½ cup chopped onion
1 tsp. chopped garlic
1½ tsp. ground cumin
6 cups shredded cabbage
Pepper to taste, *optional*

1. Heat oil in large skillet. Add mustard seeds. Heat until they start to pop.

2. Add onion and garlic. Sauté 2–3 minutes.

3. Add cumin and cabbage. Sauté, stirring every 5 minutes. Cook until cabbage is tender but not too soft.

4. Sprinkle with pepper if you wish before serving.

Serving suggestion:

This would go well with Encore Dijon Chicken on page 78 or Ginger Pork Chops on page 108.

Calories: 53
Fat: 3 g
Saturated Fat: 0 g
Carbohydrates: 6 g
Fiber: 2 g
Sodium: 14 mg
Protein: 2 g
Cholesterol: 0 mg

Apple Coleslaw

NO-COOK

Joy Uhler, Richardson, TX

Makes 9 servings, about ½ cup per serving

Prep. Time: 20 minutes

2 cups coleslaw mix

1 unpeeled apple, cored and chopped

½ cup chopped celery

½ cup chopped green pepper

½ cup chopped broccoli, *optional*

¼ cup canola oil

2 Tbsp. lemon juice

1 Tbsp. sugar-free honey

1. In a bowl, combine coleslaw mix, apple, celery, green pepper, and broccoli.

2. In a small bowl, whisk together oil, lemon juice, and honey. Pour over coleslaw and toss to coat evenly.

Variation:

Use red or yellow peppers for even more color.

Serving suggestion:

It is perfect beside salmon.

Calories: 80

Fat: 6 g

Saturated Fat: 0.5 g

Carbohydrates: 7 g

Fiber: 1 g

Sodium: 10 mg

Protein: 0.5 g

Cholesterol: 0 mg

Sweet Potato Puree

Colleen Heatwole, Burton, MI

Makes 4 servings

Prep. Time: 10 minutes ⚬ Cooking Time: 6 minutes

3 lb. sweet potatoes, peeled and cut into roughly 2-inch cubes

I cup water

2 Tbs. olive oil buttery spread

I tsp. salt

I tsp. brown sugar substitute such as Truvia Stevia Leaf Brown Sweetener

2 tsp. lemon juice

½ tsp. cinnamon

⅛ tsp. nutmeg, *optional*

1. Place sweet potatoes and water in inner pot of the Instant Pot.

2. Secure the lid, make sure vent is at sealing, then cook for 6 minutes on high using the Manual setting.

3. Manually release the pressure when cook time is up.

4. Drain sweet potatoes and place in large mixing bowl. Mash with potato masher or hand mixer.

5. Once thoroughly mashed, add remaining ingredients.

6. Taste and adjust seasonings to taste.

7. Serve immediately while still hot.

Serving suggestion:

This would go well with Pork Cutlets on page 107 or Buttery Lemon Chicken on page 74.

Calories: 239

Fat: 5 g

Saturated Fat: I g

Carbohydrates: 47 g

Fiber: 7 g

Sodium: 446 mg

Protein: 4 g

Cholesterol: 0 mg

Almond Rice

Dorothy VanDeest, Memphis, TN

Makes 8 servings, about 5–6 oz. per serving

Prep. Time: 20 minutes ⚭ *Cooking Time: 20 minutes*

2 cups Minute Brown Rice, uncooked

1 Tbsp. olive oil buttery spread

3½ cups water

4 reduced-sodium beef bouillon cubes

½ cup slivered toasted almonds

6 green onions, chopped

2½ Tbsp. reduced-sodium soy sauce

1. Mix rice and buttery spread in skillet. Sauté until rice begins to brown, stirring frequently to prevent burning.

2. In a small saucepan, bring water to a boil. Dissolve bouillon cubes in boiling water.

3. Add water to rice and mix. Cover and simmer until liquid disappears, 15–20 minutes.

4. Stir in almonds, chopped green onions, and soy sauce. Heat 1 minute longer.

Serving suggestion:

This would go well with French Onion Chicken on page 75, Nutty Salmon on page 124, or Basil Chicken Strips on page 84.

Calories: 129

Fat: 5 g

Saturated Fat: 1 g

Carbohydrates: 16 g

Fiber: 2 g

Sodium: 423 mg

Protein: 6 g

Cholesterol: 0 mg

Desserts

White Chip Pumpkin Cookies

Joanna Harrison, Lafayette, CO

Makes 60 cookies, 1 cookie per serving

Prep. Time: 15 minutes ⚬ *Baking Time: 11–14 minutes*

2 sticks (1 cup) butter
¼ cup Splenda Brown Sugar Blend
¼ cup Splenda Sugar Blend
1 egg
2 tsp. vanilla extract
1 cup cooked, puréed pumpkin
2 cups flour
1 tsp. ground cardamom
2 tsp. ground cinnamon
1 tsp. baking soda
1¼ cups white chocolate chips
⅔ cup chopped nuts, *optional*

1. Using a mixer, cream together butter, Splenda, egg, and vanilla. Beat in pumpkin.

2. Separately, stir together flour, cardamom, cinnamon, and baking soda.

3. Stir flour mixture into butter mixture. Stir in chocolate chips and optional nuts.

4. Drop spoonfuls onto greased cookie sheet.

5. Bake at 350°F for 11–14 minutes.

Calories: 72
Fat: 4 g
Saturated Fat: 3 g
Carbohydrates: 7 g
Fiber: 0 g
Sodium: 75 mg
Protein: 1 g
Cholesterol: 12 mg

OVEN

Apple-Walnut Cookies

Rhonda Burgoon, Collingswood, NJ

Makes 36 cookies; 2 cookies/serving

Prep. Time: 20 minutes & Baking Time: 10–12 minutes

1 cup dry rolled oats

½ cup chopped walnuts

1 cup whole wheat pastry flour

½ tsp. baking soda

¼ tsp. baking powder

¼ tsp. salt

½ tsp. ground cinnamon

¼ tsp. ground ginger

2 egg whites

1 Granny Smith apple peeled, cored, and grated

¼ cup unsweetened applesauce

½ cup light brown sugar, packed

2 Tbsp. canola oil

½ tsp. vanilla extract

½ cup raisins

1. Heat oven to 375°F. Spray 2 baking sheets with nonstick cooking spray.

2. Place oats and nuts on separate unsprayed baking sheets. Toast in oven until golden, about 8 minutes. Set aside.

3. Meanwhile, combine flour, baking soda, baking powder, salt, cinnamon, and ginger in a medium bowl.

4. In a large bowl, combine egg whites, grated apple, applesauce, brown sugar, oil, and vanilla.

5. Stir in combined dry ingredients until well blended.

6. Stir in raisins, oats, and nuts.

7. Drop dough onto prepared baking sheets by tablespoonfuls placed 2 inches apart.

8. Bake 10–12 minutes, or until cookies are lightly browned.

9. Cool on wire racks for 3 minutes. Cool completely before serving.

Calories: 60

Fat: 2 g

Saturated Fat: 0 g

Carbohydrates: 10 g

Fiber: 1 g

Sodium: 35 mg

Protein: 1 g

Cholesterol: 0 mg

Chocolate Peanut Butter Fudge

NO-COOK

Hope Comerford, Clinton Township, MI

Makes 16 servings (1 piece per serving)

Prep. Time: 5 minutes

½ cup coconut oil, melted

12 oz. no-sugar-added
creamy peanut butter

½ cup unsweetened cacao powder

½ cup sugar-free confectioners' sugar

1 tsp. vanilla extract

½ tsp. sea salt

1. Mix the melted coconut oil with the creamy peanut butter until well-combined.

2. Mix in the cacao powder, sugar-free confectioners' sugar, vanilla, and sea salt.

3. Line an 8 × 8-inch pan with parchment paper and spread the chocolate peanut butter mixture evenly in the pan.

4. You can place it in the freezer for about 20–25 minutes to set, or in the refrigerator for an hour or two.

Calories: 195

Fat: 14 g

Saturated Fat: 7 g

Carbohydrates: 12 g

Fiber: 2 g

Sodium: 129 mg

Protein: 5 g

Cholesterol: 0 mg

Red, White & Blue Parfait

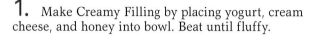

Becky Gehman, Bergton, VA

Makes 4 servings

Prep. Time: 15 minutes

Creamy Filling:

1 cup low-fat sugar-free vanilla yogurt

¼ cup fat-free cream cheese (Neufchâtel), softened

1 tsp. sugar-free honey

1 pint fresh strawberries, sliced, *divided*

1½ cups fresh blueberries, *divided*

1. Make Creamy Filling by placing yogurt, cream cheese, and honey into bowl. Beat until fluffy.

2. Assemble parfaits by placing ⅓ cup strawberries in each of 6 parfait glasses.

3. Top each with 3 Tbsp. Creamy Filling.

4. Top that with ¼ cup blueberries in each glass.

5. Garnish each by dividing remaining topping.

6. Chill until ready to serve.

Calories: 114

Fat: 4 g

Saturated Fat: 2 g

Carbohydrates: 18 g

Fiber: 3 g

Sodium: 69 mg

Protein: 5 g

Cholesterol: 14 mg

Ambrosia Parfaits

Irene Klaeger, Inverness, FL

Makes 4 servings

Prep. Time: 15 minutes

16-oz. carton low-fat sugar-free vanilla yogurt

¼ cup no-sugar-added crushed pineapple in juice, drained

1 banana, peeled and cut into ¼-inch slices

11-oz. can no-sugar-added mandarin oranges

1 Tbsp. flaked coconut, toasted

4 fresh strawberries, sliced

1. Spoon yogurt onto several layers of heavy duty paper towels and spread to ½-inch thickness. Cover with additional paper towels. Let stand 5 minutes.

2. Scrape yogurt into bowl using a rubber spatula.

3. Stir in drained pineapple.

4. Spoon 2 Tbsp. yogurt mixture into each of 4 parfait glasses.

5. Top evenly with banana slices and orange slices.

6. Dollop remaining yogurt over orange slices.

7. Sprinkle evenly with coconut.

8. Top each with sliced strawberries.

Calories: 173

Fat: 2 g

Saturated Fat: 1 g

Carbohydrates: 34 g

Fiber: 2 g

Sodium: 86 mg

Protein: 7 g

Cholesterol: 6 mg

Four-Fruit Yogurt Smoothie

Janet Oberholtzer, Ephrata, PA

Makes 4 servings

Prep. Time: 10 minutes

1 cup frozen unsweetened strawberries
1 cup frozen unsweetened peaches
¾ cup frozen unsweetened blueberries
1 large ripe banana
1 cup fat-free sugar-free peach, or strawberry, yogurt
1 cup skim milk

1. Combine all ingredients in blender or food processor.

2. Process until smooth, stopping to scrape sides and push ingredients down into blender as needed.

3. Pour into serving glasses.

Calories: 119
Fat: 0.5 g
Saturated Fat: 0.2 g
Carbohydrates: 24 g
Fiber: 3 g
Sodium: 60 mg
Protein: 5 g
Cholesterol: 2 mg

Chia Seed Pudding

MICRO-WAVE

Hope Comerford, Clinton Township, MI

Makes 4 servings

Prep. Time: 10 minutes

2 cups skim milk

¾ cup chia seeds

2½ cups fat-free sugar-free vanilla yogurt

1 cup blueberries, *divided*

1 Tbsp. sugar-free mini chocolate chips, *divided*

1. Pour the milk into a microwave-safe bowl and heat for 1½ minutes.

2. Stir in the chia seeds and let them sit for 5 minutes to thicken.

3. Stir in the yogurt.

4. Divide the chia/yogurt mixture into 4 serving dishes.

5. Top each dish with ¼ cup of the blueberries and 1 tsp. sugar-free mini chocolate chips.

Serving suggestion:

For an extra amount of deliciousness, top with a little bit of light Cool Whip.

Calories: 171

Fat: 3 g

Saturated Fat: 1 g

Carbohydrates: 27 g

Fiber: 3 g

Sodium: 137 mg

Protein: 11 g

Cholesterol: 5 mg

NO-COOK

Fruit Pudding

Penny Blosser, New Carlisle, OH
Phoebe M. Yoder, Bristol, IN

Makes 10 servings, about 5½ oz. per serving

Prep. Time: 20 minutes

8-oz. can no-sugar-added pineapple chunks, undrained

11-oz. can no-sugar-added mandarin oranges, undrained

17-oz. can fruit cocktail packed in juice, undrained

⅓ cup unsweetened coconut

2 Tbsp. lemon juice

1-oz. pkg. sugar-free fat-free lemon instant pudding

1 cup fat-free milk

2 bananas, sliced

1. Combine pineapple, mandarin oranges, fruit cocktail, coconut, and lemon juice.

2. Combine pudding and milk and mix well.

3. Combine fruit mixture with pudding mixture and stir gently to combine all ingredients.

4. Immediately before serving, fold in sliced bananas.

Calories: 93

Fat: 1 g

Saturated Fat: 1 g

Carbohydrates: 21 g

Fiber: 2 g

Sodium: 50 mg

Protein: 2 g

Cholesterol: 0 mg

Lime Poppy Seed Fruit Salad

Diann Dunham, State College, PA

Makes 4½ cups, ½ cup per serving, 9 servings total

Prep. Time: 20 minutes

2 cups no-sugar-added pineapple chunks, canned, juice reserved

1 orange, peeled and chopped

1 kiwi fruit, peeled and sliced

1 cup red or green grapes

1 cup quartered strawberries

Dressing:

¼ cup reserved pineapple juice

¼ tsp. grated lime peel

2 Tbsp. fresh lime juice

1 Tbsp. sugar-free honey

1 tsp. poppy seeds

Whole strawberries, *optional*

1. Mix pineapple chunks, orange, kiwi, grapes, and strawberries in a bowl.

2. In a separate bowl, mix dressing ingredients. Add dressing to salad.

3. If desired, garnish with a few whole strawberries before serving.

Tip:

The salad is best made and eaten the same day. Strawberries get mushy if stored too long.

Calories: 60

Fat: 0 g

Saturated Fat: 0 g

Carbohydrates: 15 g

Fiber: 2 g

Sodium: 2 mg

Protein: 1 g

Cholesterol: 0 mg

NO-COOK

Healthy Fruit Salad

Ida C. Knopp, Salem, OH

Makes 8 servings, about ½ cup per serving

Prep. Time: 15 minutes

3 tart red apples, chopped

3 oranges, chopped

½ cup chopped celery

⅓ cup raisins

⅓ cup chopped nuts

2 Tbsp. sugar-free honey

2 Tbsp. lemon juice

1. In a serving bowl toss apples, oranges, celery, raisins, and nuts.

2. In a small bowl combine honey and lemon juice. Drizzle over fruit salad and serve.

Calories: 125

Fat: 3 g

Saturated Fat: 0 g

Carbohydrates: 25 g

Fiber: 3 g

Sodium: 7 mg

Protein: 2 g

Cholesterol: 0 mg

Extra Information

If you're accustomed to using metric measurements, I don't want you to be inconvenienced by the imperial measurements I use in this book.

Weight (Dry Ingredients)

1 oz		30 g
4 oz	¼ lb	120 g
8 oz	½ lb	240 g
12 oz	¾ lb	360 g
16 oz	1 lb	480 g
32 oz	2 lb	960 g

Length

¼ in	6 mm
½ in	13 mm
¾ in	19 mm
1 in	25 mm
6 in	15 cm
12 in	30 cm

Volume (Liquid Ingredients)

½ tsp.		2 ml
1 tsp.		5 ml
1 Tbsp.	½ fl oz	15 ml
2 Tbsp.	1 fl oz	30 ml
¼ cup	2 fl oz	60 ml
⅓ cup	3 fl oz	80 ml
½ cup	4 fl oz	120 ml
⅔ cup	5 fl oz	160 ml
¾ cup	6 fl oz	180 ml
1 cup	8 fl oz	240 ml
1 pt	16 fl oz	480 ml
1 qt	32 fl oz	960 ml

Recipe & Ingredient Index

Recipe & Ingredient Index 213

About the Author

Hope Comerford is a mom, wife, elementary music teacher, blogger, recipe developer, public speaker, Young Living Essential Oils essential oil enthusiast/ educator, and published author. In 2013, she was diagnosed with a severe gluten intolerance and since then has spent many hours creating easy, practical, and delicious gluten-free recipes that can be enjoyed by both those who are affected by gluten and those who are not.

Growing up, Hope spent many hours in the kitchen with her Meme (grandmother) and her love for cooking grew from there. While working on her master's degree when her daughter was young, Hope turned to her slow cookers for some salvation and sanity. It was from there she began truly experimenting with recipes and quickly learned she had the ability to get a little more creative in the kitchen and develop her own recipes.

In 2010, Hope started her blog, *A Busy Mom's Slow Cooker Adventures*, to simply share the recipes she was making with her family and friends. She never imagined people all over the world would begin visiting her page and sharing her recipes with others as well. In 2013, Hope self-published her first cookbook, *Slow Cooker Recipes 10 Ingredients or Less and Gluten-Free*, and then later wrote *The Gluten-Free Slow Cooker*.

Hope became the new brand ambassador and author of Fix-It and Forget-It in mid-2016. Since then, she has brought her excitement and creativeness to the Fix-It and Forget-It brand. Through Fix-It and Forget-It, she has written *Fix-It and Forget-It Instant Pot Diabetic Cookbook, Fix-It and Forget-It Healthy Slow-Cooker Cookbook, Fix-It and Forget-It Big Book of Keto Recipes, Welcome Home Diabetic Cookbook, Fix-It and Forget-It Plant-Based Comfort Food Cookbook,* and many more.

Hope lives in the city of Clinton Township, Michigan, near Metro Detroit. She has been happily married to her husband and best friend, Justin, since 2008. Together they have two children, Ella and Gavin, who are her motivation, inspiration, and heart. In her spare time, Hope enjoys traveling, singing, cooking, reading books, spending time with friends and family, and relaxing.

Also Available!

NEW YORK TIMES BESTSELLING SERIES

FIX-IT and FORGET-IT®

INSTANT POT

DIABETES

COOKBOOK

HOPE COMERFORD

127 SUPER EASY HEALING RECIPES